SALES TRAINING

Further titles in the McGraw-Hill Training Series

THE BUSINESS OF TRAINING
Achieving Success in Changing World Markets
Trevor Bentley   ISBN 0-07-707328-2

EVALUATING TRAINING EFFECTIVENESS
Translating Theory into Practice
Peter Bramley   ISBN 0-07-707331-2

DEVELOPING EFFECTIVE TRAINING SKILLS
Tony Pont   ISBN 0-07-707383-5

MAKING MANAGEMENT DEVELOPMENT WORK
Achieving Success in the Nineties
Charles Margerison   ISBN 0-07-707382-7

MANAGING PERSONAL LEARNING AND CHANGE
A Trainer's Guide
Neil Clark   ISBN 0-07-707344-4

HOW TO DESIGN EFFECTIVE TEXT-BASED OPEN LEARNING:
A Modular Course
Nigel Harrison   ISBN 0-07-707355-X

HOW TO DESIGN EFFECTIVE COMPUTER BASED TRAINING:
A Modular Course
Nigel Harrison   ISBN 0-07-707354-1

HOW TO SUCCEED IN EMPLOYEE DEVELOPMENT
Moving from Vision to Results
Ed Moorby   ISBN 0-07-707459-9

DEVELOPING WOMEN THROUGH TRAINING
A Practical Handbook
Liz Willis and
Jenny Daisley   ISBN 0-07-707566-8

USING VIDEO IN TRAINING AND EDUCATION
Ashly Pinnington   ISBN 0-07-707384-3

TRANSACTIONAL ANALYSIS
A Handbook for Trainers
Julie Hay   ISBN 0-07-707470-X

Details of these and other titles in the series are available from:

The Product Manager, Professional Books, McGraw-Hill Book Company Europe,
Shoppenhangers Road, Maidenhead, Berkshire, SL6 2QL.
Telephone: 0628 23432 Fax: 0628 770224

Sales training

A guide to developing effective salespeople

Frank S Salisbury

McGRAW-HILL BOOK COMPANY

London · New York · St Louis · San Francisco · Auckland
Bogotá · Caracas · Hamburg · Lisbon · Madrid · Mexico · Milan
Montreal · New Delhi · Panama · Paris · San Juan · São Paulo
Singapore · Sydney · Tokyo · Toronto

Published by
McGRAW-HILL Book Company Europe
Shoppenhangers Road, Maidenhead, Berkshire, SL6 2QL, England.
Telephone: 0628 23432
Fax: 0628 770224

British Library Cataloguing in Publication Data
Salisbury, Frank S.
  Sales Training: Guide to Developing
  Effective Salespeople. (McGraw-Hill
  Training Series)
  I. Title II. Series
  658.3

  ISBN 0-07-707458-0

Library of Congress Cataloging-in-Publication Data
Salisbury, Frank.
  Sales training: a guide to developing effective salespeople /
Frank S. Salisbury
     p.   cm.
  Includes bibliographical references and index.
  ISBN 0-07-707458-0
  1. Sales personnel—Training of.   I. Title.
HF5439.8.S36   1992
658.3'1245—dc20   91–45605
                                                               CIP

12345 CL 95432

Typeset by Book Ens Limited, Baldock, Herts
Printed and bound in Great Britain by Clays Ltd, St Ives plc

To Pauline who put up with the lost hours, corrected my work, and supported my ambition to write this book.

To Michael and Helen who seemed to grow up too quickly during the eight years it took.

To Billy, dearly loved and sorely missed.

Contents

Contents

Series preface

Training and development are now firmly centre stage in most organizations, if not all. Nothing unusual in that—for some organizations. They have always seen training and development as part of the heart of their businesses—but more and more must see it that same way.

The demographic trends through the nineties will inject into the marketplace severe competition for good people who will need good training. Young people without conventional qualifications, skilled workers in redundant crafts, people out of work, women wishing to return to work—all will require excellent training to fit them to meet the job demands of the 1990s and beyond.

But excellent training does not spring from what we have done well in the past. T&D specialists are in a new ball game. 'Maintenance' training—training to keep up skill levels to do what we have always done—will be less in demand. Rather, organization, work and market change training are now much more important and will remain so for some time. Changing organizations and people is no easy task, requiring special skills and expertise which, sadly, many T&D specialists do not possess.

To work as a 'change' specialist requires us to get to centre stage—to the heart of the company's business. This means we have to ask about future goals and strategies and even be involved in their development, at least as far as T&D policies are concerned.

This demands excellent communication skills, political expertise, negotiating ability, diagnostic skills—indeed, all the skills a good internal consultant requires.

The implications for T&D specialists are considerable. It is not enough merely to be skilled in the basics of training, we must also begin to act like business people and to think in business terms and talk the language of business. We must be able to resource training not just from within but by using the vast array of external resources. We must be able to manage our activities as well as any other manager. We must share in the creation and communication of the company's vision. We must never let the goals of the company out of our sight.

In short, we may have to grow and change with the business. It will be hard. We shall not only have to demonstrate relevance but also value for money and achievement of results. We shall be our own boss, as accountable for results as any other line manager, and we shall have to deal with fewer internal resources.

The challenge is on, as many T&D specialists have demonstrated to me over the past few years. We need to be capable of meeting that challenge. This is why McGraw-Hill Book Company Europe have planned and launched this major new training series—to help us meet that challenge.

The series covers all aspects of T&D and provides the knowledge base from which we can develop plans to meet the challenge. They are practical books for the professional person. They are a starting point for planning our journey into the twenty-first century.

Use them well. Don't just read them. Highlight key ideas, thoughts, action pointers or whatever, and have a go at doing something with them. Through experimentation we evolve; through stagnation we die.

I know that all the authors in the McGraw-Hill Training Series would want me to wish you good luck. Have a great journey into the twenty-first century.

ROGER BENNETT
Series Editor

About the series editor

Roger Bennett has over 20 years' experience in training, management education, research and consulting. He has long been involved with trainer training and trainer effectiveness. He has carried out research into trainer effectiveness and conducted workshops, seminars and conferences on the subject around the world. He has written extensively on the subject including the book *Improving Trainer Effectiveness*, Gower. His work has taken him all over the world and has involved directors of companies as well as managers and trainers.

Roger Bennett has worked in engineering, several business schools (including the International Management Centre, where he launched the UK's first masters degree in T&D) and has been a board director of two companies. He is the editor of the *Journal of European Industrial Training* and was series editor of the ITD's *Get In There* workbook and video package for the managers of training departments. He now runs his own business called The Management Development Consultancy.

Preface

Sales training is not a package that you can pick up off the shelf, and it does not work on its own. It should be viewed as an integral part of your company's total managerial strategy, not something to be turned on when there is a need and turned off when resources are scarce. You either believe in it or you do not. There are no half measures.

This book is meant to stimulate you into changing the way in which training, and especially sales training, is viewed in most companies. It should encourage and stimulate discussion about the role of the trainer and the role of the manager. The first few chapters centre on the fundamental reasons why sales training fails to deliver and how sales trainers should be involved more in the running of the business. The natural tendency will be to delve into the later chapters which are more concerned with the 'how' than with the 'why', but I must emphasize that unless you resolve the 'why' then the 'how' will not really matter.

I am determined that selling, sales management and sales training should achieve a far higher professional profile than exists at present. It concerns me that so many people work in the industry of selling in various roles, and yet the reputation of selling, sales management and sales training has no professional standing. A great deal of it has to do with the attitude of people working in the industry; in more than twenty years in selling I have found a wasteland of professional achievement and a lack of professionalism in selling. I hope this book will contribute something to the aim of creating a professional standard for selling and in particular for the salesperson and the sales trainer. This book also represents the first of several books I am writing on the subject of selling, the next two dealing with sales management and personal selling itself.

Like most people in selling, I left school not wanting to be a salesman. I was not sure what I wanted to be, but I was certain that I did not want to be a salesman. The other thing I did not want to do was to become a tax-payer. It was not long before I failed miserably on both counts. I got into selling by accident. The company I joined called it merchandizing. It did not fool me nor anyone else. It was not long before I was promoted to a sales management role, and the response from people I knew was that they were pleased I had got out of selling and into management. Sorry to relate, so was I.

I have spent more of my life in selling than out of it and some years ago I determined that my life was worth something more than feeling self-conscious about what I felt was a profession but no one else did. I became determined to become professionally qualified in the specific area of selling, not through joining an association or seeking fellowship of a selling institute, but by taking the process head on and doing it academically. In 1990 I completed six years of academic research and this book is the culmination of a dream I had in 1982 to write a sales book that was based on research and would contribute significantly to the industry of selling.

The book is meant, first, to be read as a whole and then used as reference material for ideas. The only way in which you will enhance your own job prospects, however, and get the same sense of professional achievement that I have gained is to use it as a stimulus for creating your own ideas. You will also probably recognize that there is little new in selling, sales management or sales training, merely different ways of packaging the same message. I found that many of the processes used in training are as old as selling itself. The problem is that, along the way, the research backing up most of the claims made on sales training programmes has been lost or deliberately left out. I think this is a pity from two viewpoints. Good quality research can only enhance the delivery and effectiveness of training and, secondly, it gives it credibility.

I believe this book will quickly show you that the ideas and suggestions contained in its pages are both credible and practical. I do not underestimate the problems you will encounter with some of the basic principles, especially with regard to the initial chapters on structure, policy, and training needs identification. Nothing worth having, however, is achieved without effort and pain.

I encourage you to promote the profession of selling in a professional manner. Encourage your managers to become professionally qualified and your salespeople to study the world's oldest profession—selling. This book can only be a foundation stone in building a professional sales, sales training and sales management career, and if it achieves that it will have achieved what I set out to do.

Acknowledgements

At this point I should mention some people to whom I owe an unpaid debt of thanks and eternal gratitude, and to two in particular.

First is a New Zealander called Alan Pashby whom I met in the Spring of 1981. Alan rekindled in me a spark that had gone out many years before. I would place him as one of the greatest stand-up sales trainers I have ever heard or seen. He had the gift of motivating people towards excellence, a quality that is rare among trainers.

Second is Ian Barrett. I knew him for only a short time between 1987 and 1988 but he gave me a lifetime of confidence and belief in my own talent and skills. He died tragically in 1988 and is sorely missed.

It is a sad indictment of the training industry that in more than twenty years of selling I met only two people who embodied the greatness of all that is the professional sales trainer.

I would like to thank Roger Bennett who helped me through my DMS, set me on the path to academia and supported my MPhil. I also owe a debt to Professor Trevor Watkins of Oxford Polytechnic without whom my research would probably not have reached its successful conclusion.

Thank you to the team at McGraw Hill. In particular Jenny Ertle, Linda Mitchell, Lavinia Porter, and James Hyde.

Lastly, I am indebted to all the salespeople I know who formed the basis of my research. It is to their efforts, successes and failures that I and all my peers owe their livelihood.

Frank S Salisbury

1 Selling and salesmanship

This chapter gives an overview of selling, salespeople and sales training and describes the image that selling has acquired over the centuries.

Background

'Sales training doesn't work', said Jack Snader in 1984 and I am inclined to agree with him. That is not to say that it cannot work. It is just that in many organizations, especially those new to selling roles, like banks and building societies, the environment does not allow for it to work. If my own experience is anything to go by then most sales training carried out in this country is non-effective. Yes, it works in classrooms and, yes, trainers and their managers can provide evaluations which show that it works. In the field, however, in branches and shops, in real life, it does not work.

Only the other day my wife and I went into a branch of a major retailer who spends millions of pounds on customer care and sales training programmes and found it impossible to part with money. We were prepared to spend £3000 on furniture but were unable to excite anyone sufficiently to take it. We left after about twenty minutes during which time it became clear that our desire to buy was a distraction during stocktaking and form-filling. You and I both know that this is no isolated incident. Selling as an activity seems to have died. Where are the salespeople? Millions of consumers are waiting to be sold to. Why does sales training appear to fail?

A clue to the fact that sales training does fail is the number of firms offering sales training solutions. During the last ten years there has been an explosion in the number of consultancies offering sales training. Equally, the number of specialist salespeople recruitment agencies has mushroomed. The latter have obviously realized that sales training does not work and therefore the solution to sales success must lie in recruiting good salespeople in the first place. Companies are as susceptible to buying recruitment packages as they are to buying sales training packages.

I believe that current sales training in the majority of British organizations is positively harmful to employee performance. A good deal of nonsense tends to be talked about selling and sales training, either by those who have not been in selling themselves or by people better suited to any career other than selling or sales training.

In a sales career spanning more than twenty years I have participated in numerous sales training courses, first as a trainee and then as a trainer. During this time I was presented with many different views on selling and sales training, each one seemingly offering a new insight. In time, however, I began to question the validity of much of what was on offer and in delving deeper found some approaches to be shallow and devoid of substance. Others were very similar to each other.

Some people say that salespeople are born, and for a long time my own success seemed to bear this out. Without any formal sales training I found I could make a good living and was eventually encouraged to train others. What I found disturbing was that, while some of my colleagues enjoyed success, large numbers continued to fail. In reality I scored some notable failures myself even after (eventually) receiving some professional sales training. Looking around, I found this picture of sales failure was repeated everywhere. There are more salespeople failing each day than there are succeeding. A thorough evaluation of most sales training programmes will reveal to you that current sales training courses appear to contribute to sales failure rather than to have a positive effect on performance.

Sales trainers and sales managers put the level of failure down to a lack of commitment or poor material in the first place. Failed salespeople put failure down to bad luck. My research has shown that:

1 There seems to be nothing new in sales training, just novel ways of packaging the same material. The basic structure of sales present-ations taught on training courses follows a remarkably similar pattern, no matter what industry you look at or which company you investigate, as does the teaching of techniques for overcoming objectives and closing the sale.
2 Selling appears to be a lot simpler than some trainers and writers make it out to be.
3 It is an honourable profession with a dishonourable reputation.
4 Some people do it naturally without formal training.
5 No one person has yet come up with the magic formula for sales suc-cess. This, however, does not stop salespeople believing that there is one, and has created a supply from those who think they have the answer.

Perhaps the answer is really more straightforward. 'The biggest problem with sales training,' a new recruit told me recently, 'is that they tell you how to overcome objections, and how to close the sale, but then that isn't difficult anyway. What they never tell you is where to find the people to sell to in the first place.'

What is selling?

It was Robert Louis Stevenson who said 'Everyone lives by selling something' and whether you define selling as being the act of trading, bartering or simply exchanging goods or services, it is obvious that it has been with us a long time. It could be said that the first great salesperson, if person is the right description, was the serpent in the Garden of Eden—'Listen, Eve, what I've got here will blow your mind. Not only will it be better than boring gardening but also it is free.' Centuries later consumers are still being sold the 'no strings, interest free' message. Its seemingly perpetual existence, however, seems not to have made it any more acceptable, and perhaps the fact that the Devil was the first truly great salesman is part of the reason. While the word 'selling' seems easy enough to understand, most comprehensive dictionaries also offer insights into what people really think about selling. It is described as involving trickery or deception. The ancient Roman word for salesman meant 'cheater' and Plato referred to the early salesman as someone who, in a well-run community, was fit for little else. The sad and negative image of the salesman was most pointedly exemplified by Arthur Miller's play *Death of a Salesman*. Willy Loman, or his clone, appears continually in films and plays where the salesman has a part—unless it is comedy, in which case Michael Crawford's role as Frank Spencer takes precedence. Most recently we have 'Del Boy', the archetypal salesman played by David Jason in *Only Fools and Horses*. This role, while humorous without doubt, confirms many people's belief that salespeople are out to con you. Their mission in life is to move as many poor quality goods as quickly as possible, at the maximum profit. It would be wrong of me not to admit that it does happen, for it does. Equally, however, there are far more salespeople trying to provide their customers with something they believe in, and something that will benefit both supplier and consumer.

Vast sums are spent yearly trying to improve the image of the salesman. In the early 1950s, selling, having failed to emerge as an honourable profession, became part of a far more acceptable description—'the marketing executive'. This term 'marketing' suggests that organizations have researched what is wanted by whom, and that goods and services are created to supply that demand. Selling, in comparison, is directed towards providing customers with things they do not need but are persuaded to buy. It is from the peddlers and bagmen of the seventeenth, eighteenth and nineteenth centuries that many of the current attitudes towards salespeople emerged. Plato was not far from the truth in his description. It was agriculture that was always seen as the most honourable of professions. The earliest salespeople were employed only as a last resort, because farmers were unable to secure regular deliveries of their produce to the marketplace without the intervention of a middleman. The modern salesman is epitomized by the American bagman, a hard-working, hard-drinking, ruthless character, updated in such roles as Gordon Gekko in the film *Wall Street*.

Definitions of selling abound. To me selling is about:

- Identifying qualified buyers who will purchase your product or service;
- Selling yourself and your company's image to those potential buyers;

• Through a process of identification of needs and wants, agreeing upon a course of action that is profitable to both parties.

Identifying qualified buyers

Most people refer to this as prospecting, and customers as prospects. Even this terminology can upset some. A colleague I used to work with refused steadfastly to believe that we were in selling; he preferred to call it marketing, and would turn purple when I called potential customers 'prospects'. If I was feeling really evil I would refer to them as 'punters'. While this description is more usually found in racing circles, perhaps it does after all describe the gamble of dealing with some salespeople. Whichever way you look at it, prospecting is the easiest topic for trainers to teach, but the most difficult of things for salespeople to do. It is the major reason for the failure of sales training, where prospecting tends to be glossed over or simplified to the extent that it appears unimportant. The usual cry from trainers and managers is: 'If we knew how to get in front of prospects, we wouldn't need to employ salespeople in the first place!'

As in most of the statements heard on courses and read in sales and training books, there is a lot of truth in that. For me, though, this attitude only helps to decry what selling is about. I do believe that Stevenson is right. We all sell, we all have something to sell and we all *have* to sell. There is nothing wrong with selling; in fact, it is selling that separates us from the passivity of animals. In truth, even animals sell themselves in order to survive. What else can mating displays be other than sales technique? Isn't this behaviour prospecting, and without prospecting how would each sex in the species be attracted to the product? I mentioned the Garden of Eden earlier. Wasn't Eve the first person to use mating displays in selling the product, in her case the apple? Watch commercial television any evening of the week, and you are guaranteed to be sold something using the 'come-hither' approach. What is this but prospecting?

And yet in sales training, prospecting seems to be regarded as the sole responsibility of the salesperson. The new recruit I mentioned earlier was right—most sales trainers do spend a lot of time training people how to overcome objections and how to close, but they never tell you how to prospect. Why?

I think it is psychological. There is something about having to prospect, or find people to buy your product or service, that reminds us of the first *big* sale—the apple, and the accompanying sin. Perhaps it is a belief that it is prospecting which is unacceptable behaviour, not selling as such. Whatever it is, prospecting has to be taught, and its role in the sales process needs to be emphasized to the extent that as much time is spent teaching people how to prospect as is spent on dealing with prospects.

Selling yourself

A great deal of work has been done on the acceptability of the individual salesperson as prime motivator in the sales process. Without doubt, princes make a better initial impression than frogs, and in the game of selling it has to be recognized that the sales process depends on the impression the salesperson makes on the prospect. If customers are motivated to buy your products in the first place, then there is indeed no need for salespeople, unless you want to increase sales. In selling, what you are saying is that people are not naturally sufficiently motivated either to buy your unique product, or to differentiate between your product and that of your competitor.

It seems a pointless exercise training people how to sell, when they first need to be taught how to dress properly and to speak good English. First impressions are paramount, and some people just make the wrong first impression. A lot of sales training fails because the people receiving the training are totally unsuitable in the first place. The most important sale in the sales presentation is the selling of yourself. That means packaging and presenting your message in the best possible light. Yet many salespeople completely ignore the fact that appearance is important. Sales trainers have a vital role to play in making trainees aware of the fact that greasy hair, beer bellies, rotten teeth, bad breath, muddy shoes, and the inability to string a sentence together in English will only come in handy if you are selling to fat, unkempt, bad-mouthed buyers.

Does this sound over the top? I can guarantee that I can walk into a number of training rooms in each town, up and down the country, and find people being taught to sell, who, even if they were given sub-machine guns as sales tools, would fail to sell life jackets to drowning men. So why do it? The reason is that too many trainers and sales managers believe that sales training is about learning how to overcome objections, and knowing when to close. I believe that there is only one objection: 'I don't like you and there's nothing here for me'. Prospects, however, have been taught not to be rude, and there is only one close—and it is made by the prospect—'Can I have some of that, please?' We will deal with this in more detail later, but for now I cannot overemphasize the need for sales trainers to concentrate on the thorny subject of 'selling yourself' in the sales process.

Needs/wants and mutual profit

Marketing has taught us all about supplying products and services that match customer needs. In many marketing books selling is seen as a process of foisting things on people who do not need them. But if a law was passed removing all the items on sale or marketed that people do not need, the shops in the West would resemble those seen in the Eastern bloc, so vividly shown on our television screens post-*glasnost*. If we all relied on people buying only what they need, we would all starve. Does anybody *need* those little gadgets seen in a host of small publications that come with our credit card bills? Do we really *need* flavoured crisps? If personal organizers in leather binders were just what we all needed, how is it that so many of them now reside un-updated in thousands of bottom drawers in executive desks? It is a well-kept secret of most successful salespeople that giving people what they want is more profitable than supplying what they need.

There is nothing wrong with making a profit. In fact, it is necessary, for profit comes before service. Unless your company makes a profit it will not be around to offer a service. The only people operating a service without profit are in the Social Services, and unless your company and thousands like it make profits to pay taxes, even the Social Services would not be in business. The other thing is that people being sold to are not stupid. They understand that your salespeople will profit from the transaction. They understand that there is no such thing as a free lunch. Even those having free lunches on the Costa del Sol and looking around thousands of empty sun-bleached villas have a slight idea that perhaps something is being sold, and a profit will be made.

Sometimes sales trainers appear to divorce buying from selling. It is as though salespeople are not also consumers. My experience tells me that salespeople are probably the easiest people in the world to sell to. They understand what it is like not to sell, and try to help the sale along. Sales trainers should accept that prospects are constantly weighing up how much profit they will make out of the sale compared with the salesperson. It is the salesperson's job to be honest about their expectation to profit from the sale and to highlight the reciprocal profit, real or perceived, that the prospect will make. There is a tendency to trust people who admit that they are in business to make profits more than those who hide behind woolly service statements. As well as asking themselves 'What's in it for me?' people also ask themselves 'What's in it for you?'

Sales training

In its simplest terms sales training can be said to train people to carry out the three elements discussed above—identifying qualified buyers, selling yourself, and determining needs and wants in order to make a profit. Instead of which, most sales training I have seen seems to contrive to encourage failure by teaching salespeople 1001 ways to con the customer into buying something they do not want. Granted, the training is gift-wrapped and called 'customer care' or 'the psychology of selling', but it still concentrates on teaching how to overcome objections and using closing techniques. In reality this is just what salespeople want. When I surveyed 200 salespeople during my research the vast majority, under 'selling skills' in the questionnaire, wanted to know how to close. In classrooms around the country sales trainers spend endless hours answering as many customer objections as salespeople can dream up, and to what end?

There seems little doubt that sales technique works. Shows like 'That's Life' in the UK have clearly demonstrated how susceptible the public is to sales technique. That said, I also believe that large sections of the public are gullible when faced with poor sales technique or even no sales technique. Some people just seem determined to buy things they don't need, want, or can afford. Perhaps there is a sales trainers' club that knows this already and puts this buying process down to their sales training. It is certain that no one can dispute it and that is the problem.

Qualified research into the effectiveness of sales training is thin on the ground. Some does exist, as does research into recruitment techniques such as the use of personality questionnaires. Yet all are published with the aim of selling something. Even this book is for sale. Perhaps Stevenson is right after all.

Selling is a much debated activity and sales training varies in its attempt to satisfy everyone's differing views and theories on what makes a good salesperson. If we truly understood what made a good salesperson then we could be more objective in what training was required. Some material appears to suggest that a good way to start would be to follow the advice of people like Frank Bettger, or Alfred Tack, who both became millionaires in sales careers and lived to tell us the tale. Or Tom Hopkins who had similar success and looks upon selling as an art rather than a science to be learnt.

Little regard is paid, however, to being in the right place at the right time, having the basic personality that allows the individual to get along with most people, or even dishonesty as a percursor to sales success. 'Con' men are a good example of this.

My definition of sales training is: 'Training which is given to those responsible for identifying and approaching prospective customers, and selling them the goods and services of the company, and which contributes directly towards the success of those potential sales'.

No definition of sales training should omit an element of the effectiveness of the training. Later in this book I discuss the pros and cons of evaluating sales training.

Retailing versus selling

Throughout this book I refer to selling as a pro-active activity, whereas retailing I distinguish as a service function. Within this distinction lies the major problem with sales training in most retailing organizations and the main reason why it fails. Not everybody wants to be a salesperson and no amount of sales training will make them into salespeople.

If you are responsible for training salespeople in a retail organization and this is the only message you get from this book, then it will have been worth the money. Unless you identify those people who want to be salespeople and therefore want sales training, *before* you give them sales training, it will not work. However, it is not quite as simple as that. Just because people say 'Yes, we want to be salespeople and we want sales training', it does not necessarily signify that they mean it. Some people just like the idea of making more money or obtaining a better benefit package. In some cases you might not have given them any choice, by threatening redundancy or company collapse if everyone did not pull together. Most major organizations manage to introduce whatever training they think fit because most employees know very well it will not change anything and, anyway, it will probably mean a couple of days off. Oh yes, and just to make sure we get more time off, we'll give the course and the trainer a jolly good rating.

Sales training has become a very complicated commodity. Now that the psychologists have entered the arena it promises to get worse and considerably more expensive. These new companies in the field of sales training are not averse to using sales technique themselves. They might say when selling their services:

'What you have to decide, Mr Sales Training Manager, is do you want something that is cheap or something of quality that is effective?'

It is a question few training managers can resist and it is usually at this point that the greatest sale of all is made. Sales training is no mystical process. It has a jargon which appears to make it so, but in essence it is about the use of inter-personal skills combined with a requisite amount of confidence building. It is confidence building that those not in selling perhaps feel uncomfortable with. However, it should be recognized that pro-active personal selling has an in-built stress element for the salesperson. The trainer's, and ultimately the manager's, job is to help the salesperson cope with that stress.

References

Miller, A. *Death of a Salesman*, Penguin 1961.
Snader, J.R. *Why most Sales Training doesn't work*, Business Marketing, May 1984.

2 Positioning of the training department

This chapter aims to answer the following questions:

- What are the current problems affecting sales training?
- What type of training departments are there in existence? Are there any recommendations for a different style?
- What is the connection between personnel and training functions and how do they work together?

In my experience both selling and sales training tend to be viewed as part of the price organizations have to pay for being in business. It is the part that involves unpalatable practices. Companies, especially those new to the idea that they have to sell themselves, would much prefer to rely upon marketing. Many salespeople now call themselves marketing executives. Marketing produces goods and services that people want to buy. It does not involve selling or if it does then selling is a small part of marketing. Even in those organizations that talk about selling and sales roles, what they really mean is marketing. When companies talk about their marketing strategy what they are really saying is: 'Is there any way we can move these goods and services without employing those nasty salespeople?' and 'If, God forbid, we have to employ salespeople, then make sure they are in minor roles and kept far away from any power base'.

Obviously, this is an exaggeration and yet there might be some truth in it when you examine the top structure in much of British industry. Corporate life in Britain is still run by accountants and finance directors and has been so since the 1960s. The source of all human endeavour and growth before this period was, in the main, ordinary people and usually salespeople at that. My research into the history of selling clearly shows that excellence and strength in corporate progress come from the ranks of salespeople and it is to be hoped that the current decline of the salesperson and sales manager is a passing phase.

Sales training: problems

Training as a company function is a new phenomenon dating from the 1960s. Its inclusion in the company balance sheet is of even greater concern than that of the salesperson. Finance directors look upon the sales function as an expense. The saviour of British industry is technology. It has given the company's senior managers a new toy to play with and with a little imagination and determination may also herald the collapse of the sales function altogether. It would appear that the tomorrow of the remote consumer using computer terminals cannot come too soon.

Your position as a sales trainer, therefore, comes at the end of a long queue and your influence on company strategy will suffer accordingly. This becomes a vicious circle for, unless the trainer is involved at the highest level in the company, the expenditure on sales training will be wasted. It will become impossible to justify the money spent on sales training if you cannot also implement the systems necessary to make sales training work. Of course, many sales trainers currently carry out evaluations showing that their training works and that objectives are exceeded. Later, in Chapter 9, I will discuss how pointless most current sales training evaluations are.

Two important questions arise about the usual positioning of training departments:

1 Why is it that most of the best trainers end up having to leave the company in order to sell their services back to that company at considerably more than their previous salary?

It is amazing how much companies are prepared to pay former employees in consultancy fees rather than pay them what they were worth in the first place. The argument for using consultants is that the tap can be turned off when either the need has gone or resources are scarce. This is a major problem in determining where sales training is positioned in the hierarchy of a company. There is a general feeling that sales training needs to be cheap if it is internal.

The most important concept you have to sell to your company is that, if they want sales training, then it must be on-going and they must pay the trainer the true rate for the job. This is fundamental to your success and the success of the sales training you carry out.

2 Why is it that sales training has to justify itself?

Training is viewed as a cost. You need to sell sales training as an investment. Marketing, finance, personnel, production—they all run the business. In many UK companies sales training is an expense, and if you need to save money it is definitely worth considering scrapping the sales training budget altogether. The reason for this is that unless you and your company get together and structure the sales training job as an integral part of the firm's existence then it will all have been a waste of money.

There is a new vogue in companies for training departments to be profit centres and sell their services to other departments. It is suggested sometimes that they should bid against external agencies in the provision of training. In many companies managers have complete discretion about who gets sales training, if any, and whether internal or external sources are used.

If you work in this sort of environment as a sales trainer then you either have to change it before you do anything else or find another company worthy of your talents. This sort of arrangement shows that your company is not serious about sales training and will probably never understand how to make it work. The same companies do not allow such discretion in deciding which finance department to use, which marketing strategy to adopt, or indeed which managers to employ. It is quite alarming how much management time is spent discussing and voting on which training package is to be bought and how the employees enjoyed the course, and yet if I were to suggest that a vote be taken each year on which managers to retain there would be an uproar.

You need to get your company to understand that salespeople are not born. Salespeople are created and they have to be trained. The notion that good salespeople are born is not supported by any existing evidence. Neither can it be proved that selling skills are connected with personality traits. If this were the case then we would all be using psychological testing in recruitment processes and save ourselves a lot of money in sales training. Those companies selling these instruments, and this in itself is a mushrooming industry, would have you believe that it is possible to spot good salespeople by these means. It appears to me that they have enjoyed some good sales training themselves and that their own company performance far outstrips the performance of the firms to which they sell.

The psychological testing industry is increasing because companies are questioning not only the validity of their current selection procedures but, more importantly, the worth of their sales training. The answer lies so close, within their own hands, that they fail to see it and are prone to being sold to by anyone who says 'I can help you pick the winners in the first place' or 'I can help you train your salespeople more effectively'.

It is precisely because there are neither salespeople nor sales trainers at the top of most major British companies that these instant solutions are listened to and bought in the first place.

Selling is a very simple process, and the answer to sales training effectiveness is equally uncomplicated. It is essential that you accept this view rather than be overawed by the complicated solutions that many external agencies try to sell you. You should question their motivation. This also means that your superiors should not confuse mind-stretching proposals with what is plainly obvious. At times you should recall and share the story of the Emperor's invisible clothes. The story goes that an Emperor was sold an invisible suit of new clothes by a tailor who said that only the most intelligent people could see them. Obviously, the Emperor claimed that he could see the clothes, and so did all his court. It took a child to point out that the Emperor was naked. In the land of the blind, the one-eyed man is king.

Children are possibly the best salespeople I have ever seen. They do the simple things and do them well. Ask any parent how good children are at selling. They use their full array of emotional selling techniques to blackmail parents into buying new toys and clothes and raising pocket money. Sometimes they do not even have to ask but just look. Children are masters at body language without even thinking about it.

As a sales trainer I see your task as one which seeks to help salespeople do simple things. However, it would appear that, in order to justify a budget, sales trainers have to do things which are complicated and difficult. There are indeed those who have succeeded and excelled at selling without formal training, but they are few and far between. To succeed at professional selling you have to be trained, and your training has to be constantly updated. Your managers have to understand that if they want good salespeople then they have to offer good sales training today, tomorrow, and the day after. There is no way that senior management would relax monetary controls within the company, or schedule financial accounting procedures only for Mondays, Wednesdays and Fridays. The same goes for sales training. To any company serious about selling, sales training has to be influential and a continuous process.

Types of departments

I see three types of training departments in existence, operating in a hierarchy of levels (see Figure 2.1). The following discussion begins with the least desirable situation.

Level Three

These are the course bookers. They are neither seen nor heard. All sales training is provided by external sources. The excuse is that they cannot afford their own training function. In some cases this may be understandable but not excusable. Sending your salespeople on external sales training courses should be offered as a leisure activity or in some instances a reward. It should never replace internal sales training. In Level Three departments where there are internal training staff, external sales trainers are used because the internal sales trainers are worse than useless.

If you have to send your salespeople on external sales courses because your internal sales trainers are ineffective, get rid of the trainers. Ask yourself why you are sending your salespeople on external sales training courses. If you are the manager and it is because you have no sales training department and you cannot train your salespeople yourself, then you have two choices:

1 Get some training on how to train your salespeople yourself; or
2 Get rid of yourself.

Level Three training departments are characterized by having few people, and they usually report to personnel departments. Too many personnel

	Characteristics of the department	Type of work generated	Effectiveness and costs	Accountability	Ease of operation
LEVEL 1 (seen and heard)	Small nucleus of professional trainers and management consultants. Involved in running the business. Needs identified at a strategic level. High technology to run systems and control mechanisms.	Small number of specialist courses, predominantly management skills oriented. Line managers involved in all development of staff. External training courses and consultancy discouraged.	Low cost per training day. Costs transferred to encourage self-development of staff and high level of technology. High long-term effectiveness and extreme flexibility to encompass change and new directions.	High accountability to match high profile. Regular management information produced, presenting both good and bad aspects.	High risk for trainers. Requires high level of quality and professionalism to work.
LEVEL 2 (seen, but not heard)	Large number of trainers, reporting either to personnel managers or separate departments. In some organizations a high level of professionalism. Tends to have high staff turnover. Reacts to line managers' identification of needs; rarely involved in business decision making.	Large number of internal courses generated each year; high staff take-up of events. External consultants used for management training. Dependent on professional staff; quality of work can be excellent.	Very effective in early years of department. Gradually becomes isolated from business by running irrelevant courses. Very slow to change. Expensive to run, internal and external change is painful.	Evaluations only ever done at course level which on the surface appears to assume responsibility and accountability. In reality no validation research carried out. No accountability for field results.	With high manpower resources, reasonably easy. With low resources tends to stress trainers.
LEVEL 3 (not seen, not heard)	Few people, reporting either to personnel manager or, where no personnel function exists, a training manager. Most needs identified by senior managers who tell training department to arrange appropriate courses.	All training provided by external training organizations. Exernal consultants used to effect changes in culture or new working practices. Number of courses and training days totally determined by size of training budget.	Only effective if external consultants accepted by senior managers. Tends to work on change items. High consultancy costs, high training day costs. No long-term return.	Training personnel not accountable for quality or outcome of training.	Very easy to run functions and to arrange courses.

Figure 2.1   *Training and development model*

departments know very little about sales training. It is common practice for training needs to be identified by line managers in unstructured conversations with their salespeople or, if they are forced to carry out an appraisal, at appraisal time. Appraisals are viewed as an intrusion into perfectly good working relationships and the interview itself is usually prefaced by 'Look, I've got to fill in this blasted form. So let's just get it out of the way, shall we?'

Isn't it usually the case that, in firms operating appraisal systems, there are no training needs evident two weeks *before* the year-end appraisal and a mountain of training needs five minutes *after*? And isn't it the same line managers who, when identifying the training needs in many companies for their staff, assume that they have been endowed with superior knowledge which makes them training professionals? It is. Throughout my long career in selling, sales management, and sales training I have observed that everybody and his dog believes that *they* are the training manager. If you want to run a successful and effective sales training department one of the first things you must do is establish the fact that *you* are the training manager. You are the professional trainer. It is your job to question the training needs that are identified and alter them when necessary. It is your job to determine the methods to be used in satisfying training needs and this will almost always involve line managers accepting their responsibilities for delivering field training.

The type of work generated by Level Three training departments is determined by how much money they have in the budget and how much external consultants charge. External consultants are always used to bring about change. Most managers firmly believe that the use of external consultants is a good idea when considering change because it occasions less resistance from staff than internally initiated processes. This wonderful theory has been sold to companies by external consultants who have a habit of never telling you that your company is terrific and does not need to change but insist that change is vital and best handled by external consultants.

Level Three training departments are seen to be very cost-effective and their training always works. It could be that the evaluation of training and its effectiveness is tainted by the fact that it is the external agency that carries out the evaluation, but perhaps that is too cynical. Let me just say that in twenty years of selling I have never seen an external sales training consultant produce a poor evaluation. Have you? The cost per training day is enormous and is usually explained by the oldest sales technique in the world—'You only get what you pay for'.

The training staff in Level Three departments are not accountable for the quality or effectiveness of training. They are merely responsible for spending money. They are keen to spend all their budget before the last quarter in any financial year so that they can prove they are under-resourced. The department is very easy to run, and they are usually out to lunch. If they do turn up at training events, they sit at the back and nod sagely.

Level Three training departments are a total waste of company resources. They are only better than nothing because one day a person might emerge from the department who is so ashamed of the type of training delivered that they actually do something about it.

Level Two   Many major organizations have what I call Level Two training departments. They are the course runners, and they are seen but not heard (see Figure 2.1). They have large numbers of trainers in them who either report to personnel managers or hold their own responsibility and report jointly to human resource directors. In some companies the department enjoys a good deal of autonomy and is staffed by highly professional teams. Within these teams there is a tendency for a high labour turnover. The training profession within companies is poorly paid and trainers soon become disillusioned with the amount the company is prepared to spend on consultants. They leave to set up their own businesses or seek operational roles within organizations which, while removed from full-time training, allow them to be rewarded to the level they feel they deserve. This turnover of professional training staff is costly and self-defeating but tolerated in the absence of professional advice.

Level Two training departments react to management decision making and design training solutions whatever the problem. They, like their Level Three counterparts, are not involved in corporate planning or any higher management decision-making processes. In this way they often deliver training programmes that have outrageously high expectations. These expectations are rarely fulfilled but the trainers feel unable to voice their belief that the impossible is being asked. To dissent at this stage would be to put next year's budget in jeopardy, and strength comes with the size of the budget and not the effectiveness of training delivered. Another symptom of high labour turnover is that there is a constant change in training emphasis and course content. Whatever is in vogue at the time is hotly pursued until the next fashion emerges. The rule of thumb of Level Two departments is 'change before anyone asks whether the current programme is working or not'. Queries are usually met with the riposte: 'I'm glad you asked that because we are just in the process of developing a course on that very subject. The problem is resources, and if you can support my proposals on increasing my headcount and budget, I'm sure we will be able to deliver what you need'.

Large numbers of internal courses are delivered each year with sets of glossy manuals and prospectuses lining staff shelves. External consultants are used only for management training. Managers, it is assumed, have highly developed brains which equate quality of training with highly expensive external courses.

Training programmes employing external sources to implement change and train managers are a pain for employees. All employees know that, once the manager gets back from the course, the next few months will involve all sorts of exercises requiring them to jump through a variety of hoops while the manager tries out new skills, knowledge and systems. The worst situation for employees is when the sales manager comes back with a project. Having had a jolly good time playing games with their peers, the net result of which confirms their own suspicions about their obvious leadership qualities, they then try out the techniques of the trainer on their own teams. It is usually a case of a little knowledge is a dangerous thing. For the managers, however, it is great for their egos, and for salespeople—well, sometimes it is better than working! Within sales management circles there is much kudos to be derived from attending the latest in-vogue training programme, provided it is called 'Advanced' or 'Executive' or 'Senior', or something like that.

For internal trainers, a new programme provides an opportunity to learn some new jargon. Level Two trainers speak a language all of their own. You simply cannot survive in Level Two departments if you cannot produce some jargon or point to the latest research. Whether the research exists or the jargon you use is correct matters not. Level Two trainers are into team building—a nightmare for employees, who are usually forced to play the same game after the manager has been trained. Level Two trainers love quality circles and total quality management programmes. They last for ever and sound good. Level Two trainers appreciate anything that requires the managers on their course to carry out some activity when they get back to the workplace. In fact, anything that gives trainers power over managers is welcomed because it allows trainers to get their own back on sales management's cynical attitude towards the training function.

When Level Two trainers meet they indulge in displays of posturing and try to impress each other with the latest book they have read:

A 'We are initiating the systems outlined by Watkinson in his latest book and have found that the effectiveness of managerial post-course activities is correlating to an extra 0.3 percentage points.'

B 'Yes, we tried that, but decided that Leibermann's work, recently tested in America, has proven more effective for us.'

The fact that neither has actually read anything is not important. The most important thing is to learn some new words.

It is important that any internal attempt to train managers is done at a country house and involves a highly respectable lecturer, and that agendas show lots of evening work. The latter is needed to show the troops back at the office what hell it all was. If courses for managers can be made to run into weekends then this not only pleases the troops but earns the undying admiration of the man at the top. The fact that the manager is tired when he gets back to work, probably from late-night drinking sessions (when the real learning process takes place), and therefore works inefficiently for the next few days, seems not to matter.

Depending on the professional staff employed, the quality of courses can be exceptional. The fact that ultimately they have only a minor effect on the organization appears of little concern. In the early days, however, Level Two departments are inclined to contribute significantly to the organization's growth and development. People need to feel they are being trained to do the job and developed for the future. Level Two departments provide plenty of scope for both. They do, however, in time become isolated from the business and are slow to adapt to the needs of the business. They end up delivering training which nobody needs, especially for salespeople.

In a strong internal Level Two training department the fulfilment of all training needs is seen to be the province of the professional staff trainer, which excludes the manager from the process. Nothing could be more harmful to salespeople and the relationship they have with sales managers than the perceived reluctance by the sales manager to take responsibility for training their own salespeople. Having identified the training needs, managers are quick to pass the responsibility for satisfying those needs to the professional trainer. Most managers in this type of organization, in whatever function, will relegate training to others paid to do it. This abdication by managers of the responsibility for training is the ruin of Level Two training departments, who see it as vindication for their existence without realizing that it reinforces their weakness. Employees equate the lack of managerial involvement in training as being a 'macho' sign that training is a subordinate activity that can be dumped as soon as a management role is achieved.

Level Two training is very expensive but the systems used to evaluate effectiveness always prove its worth. Evaluation is always done at course level, preferably on the course itself, so that the euphoria of a few days off work can encourage participants to believe what jolly nice people all the trainers are. Paradoxically, while external courses usually also enjoy high evaluations, on management courses the external trainer rarely escapes criticism. Deep down, managers feel that the company should get its money's worth and keep trainers on their toes.

Level Two trainers, like their Level Three colleagues, have no responsibility or accountability for the outcome of the training. They prefer that managers are not involved in their subordinates' training event so that they can say, 'Well, he was all right when he left the course. It must be the way he's managed'. A similar game is played by managers, who can also say, 'Well *I* didn't train him. I think that lot in the training department need to get a grip on reality'. These games are important for retaining the status quo.

Where Level Two departments enjoy high resources they are a joy to work in and could possibly be the best job in the company, apart from the fact that staff are poorly paid. Departments where manpower and resources are in short supply can be very difficult to work in, with high levels of stress and subsequent illness.

Level One   Level One trainers operate as internal consultants. They are both seen and heard. They are the most effective of training departments. They usually have a small nucleus of professional trainers and management consultants. They are involved in all aspects of the business and are keenly aware of their responsibilities and accountabilities in their contribution to corporate success. In profit-making organizations they are always aware of the bottom line. In addition they have the ability to see the far wider perspective of providing the company with trained personnel for future opportunities. Theirs is a finely tuned balancing act of providing quality training at a cost which does not burden the company's resources.

Training needs are identified at a senior management level. Training will only ever be effective if the department has a total understanding and close relationship with the people at the top of the company. The reason why large numbers of training departments fail to produce the goods has little to do with the quality or content of training but is due more to senior managers paying only lip service to their training departments. Level One trainers attend senior management meetings and contribute their significant professional manpower development knowledge to the company's business strategies.

The infrastructure of the department is geared to efficient and effective administration of the company's training needs through the use of high technology. They run a small number of central specialist courses that are predominantly management oriented. The only subordinate courses they run are of an induction type. Senior managers are often involved in these courses either as observers or participants. In this way, company policy and philosophy is consistently transmitted to all levels of staff. The vision and ideas of the chief executive are not diluted in their slow and laborious journey downward. Other line managers are all involved in the development of the subordinates either on courses or preferably in the field.

The use of external consultancies to deliver training is actively discouraged. Consultants are used to develop the knowledge and skills of the trainers, who in turn cascade that knowledge and skill to managers, who in their turn are tasked with passing the same onto their own teams. Teamwork is not a slogan but a practical reality.

The cost per training day is low but the quality is high. Budgets are discussed openly and senior managers are kept informed of all costs associated with the spending of the training budget and the returns obtained. Performance of staff is analysed before a training event and afterwards in the field. An example of a Level One training organization is Xerox, which was able to prove that they got a better return on investing in sales training than they achieved from any other marketing activity. Managers hold the key to the eventual effectiveness of the training by repeating a similar process in the field, time and time again.

Level One trainers have educated all managers in the company to understand that training in isolation does not work. Training can only work if managers are involved in all stages of a training programme. Training only works if it is recognized that training is a continuous process. Training can and does work when managers accept responsibility for training their own staff.

Level One departments are not judged on how many courses they run, or training days they deliver, or cost per employee training day. They are judged by their long-term contribution, and training is viewed as an investment in the company's most precious resource—people. Professional Level One trainers are responsible for the training policy and determining what methodology is used to deliver training. This also involves deciding who should deliver training.

These departments have a high retention of professional staff because they are involved and hence motivated to stay and see the fruits of their labours. This tenure pays off in long-term effective training. Because Level One trainers are involved in the business they are highly flexible and can change swiftly when required. They plan for change and welcome rather than resist it. In this way they act as a role model for other departments less willing or able to accept the challenge of new opportunities.

Level One trainers accept accountability and enjoy a high profile within the company. They let people know when they get things wrong and encourage risk taking.

Level One training is a high-risk activity and not for the weak. This book espouses Level One training and will help you create a Level One training department. It is, however, the most difficult route to choose in training and can prove exhausting. Depending on where your starting point is, it could take you years to get there and severely damage your own corporate health along the way. The chances are high that you will upset a great many people on your way to excellence and may not even see the results of your struggle. Nevertheless, the challenge will be enormous and the satisfaction of having achieved excellence will be reward enough.

Your ultimate goal as a Level One sales trainer is to have the maximum amount of sales training delivered that is possible. This can never be achieved by staff trainers and has to be carried out by line managers. Figure 2.2 shows the hierarchy of the development of a sales training culture. At the bottom level the company's policy is to employ only the 'natural born sales wonder'. This relieves them of the onerous and costly job of delivering any sales training at all. They are assisted in this process by selection and recruitment agencies, all with their own recipes for picking sales wonders.

Your company, and maybe even you, has to understand that the market for salespeople, and the supply of salespeople, are rapidly going in opposite directions. There are a hundred times more sales vacancies than there are salespeople to fill them. If you are looking to employ the

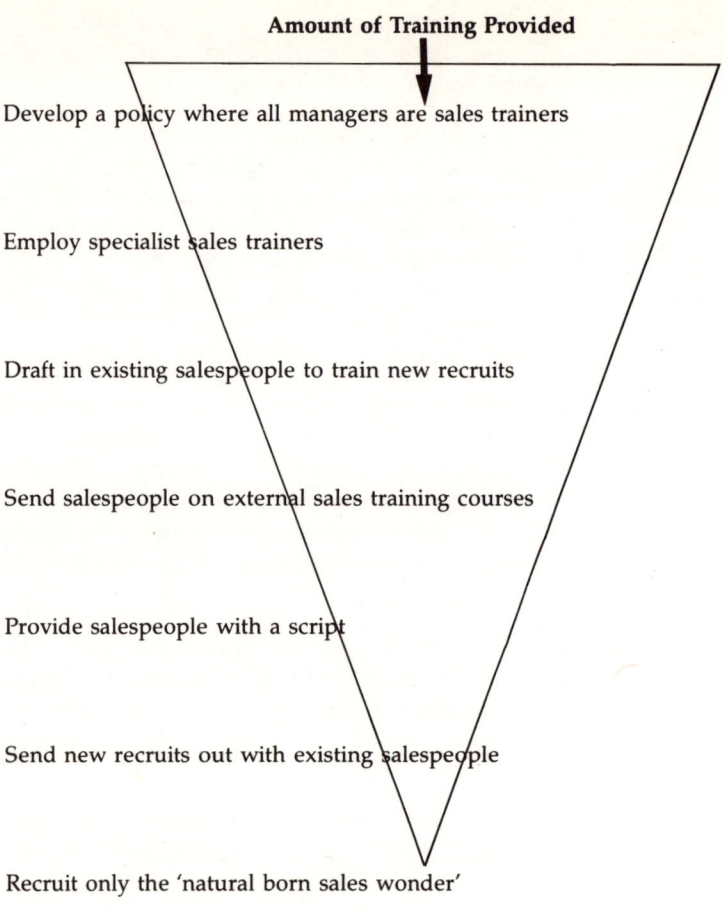

Amount of Training Provided

Develop a policy where all managers are sales trainers

Employ specialist sales trainers

Draft in existing salespeople to train new recruits

Send salespeople on external sales training courses

Provide salespeople with a script

Send new recruits out with existing salespeople

Recruit only the 'natural born sales wonder'

Figure 2.2 *Development of sales training*

natural born sales wonder then you and your company and your advisers need to think again.

Some companies send new recruits out with existing people, using the 'buddy' system. If you want your new salespeople to be just like your existing salespeople, then that's fine. If you want your new salespeople to be better than your existing salespeople then do not send them out with current salespeople. This seems obvious, but it is done. It is a cheap way of carrying out initial sales training but it does not work.

There are some companies that provide their salespeople with a script which they have to learn and repeat by heart. I knew a training consultant many years ago who told me about his first job with a major UK pharmaceutical group that provided all its salesmen with scripts. They were required to repeat the script word for word to the company's customers who in turn were contacted later to confirm that they had been told everything in the script. The reality of the situation was that many of the salesmen had built sound relationships with their customers over the years which allowed them to repeat the script and then get down to communicating properly with customers. You notice that I referred to the salesman's customers. By this I mean that, after the initial contact, using the company's name, the customer becomes the 'property' of the salesperson. It is because of the salesperson that future business comes to the company.

Further up the scale shown in Figure 2.2, some firms send their salespeople on external courses. We have already covered my views on this. Suffice it to say that these companies might as well franchise the rest of what they do too.

There are many organizations, especially in the insurance field, that draft in or second salespeople to train new recruits centrally. This has many merits and I know many companies who find that this works well. The only problem is with the motivation to return to a pro-active sales role of the salesperson returning to the field from the secondment and the resistance of the manager to releasing that salesperson into the training department in the first place.

Many of you who are training professionals will have observed the eventual loss of sales skills of sales managers caught up in the paper-work and the cosy office trap, and the same happens to seconded salespeople, although to a lesser degree. I would advise you that if a job is worth doing it is worth doing permanently on a full-time basis.

The second highest level of training activity in the hierarchy is the full-time staff sales trainer who delivers all the company's sales training either centrally or in the regions. The only danger here is the eventual divorce from reality. It is vital that this type of trainer is regularly exposed to the managers of the company to hear their feedback of the field effectiveness of the sales training delivered.

The maximum amount of sales training possible is that which fosters a sales culture in which all managers are sales trainers. The staff trainer's job is to train and support the manager. Sales training is only effective if managers are involved in all stages of development and delivery. Sales training relies on managers to make it work. Figure 2.3 shows the cyclical nature of sales training: training is initially delivered centrally; salespeople are set goals; managers are responsible both for controlling the achievement of these goals and the regular reinforcement of the central training by continuous sales training in the field.

The personnel connection

For some reason the status and image of personnel professionals have fared much better over the last twenty years than training professionals, and in many cases the sales trainer reports to the personnel manager. This is not good practice and in the majority of cases stifles the freedom of expression that the best sales trainers need. The only time that I have seen it work reasonably efficiently was where the personnel manager

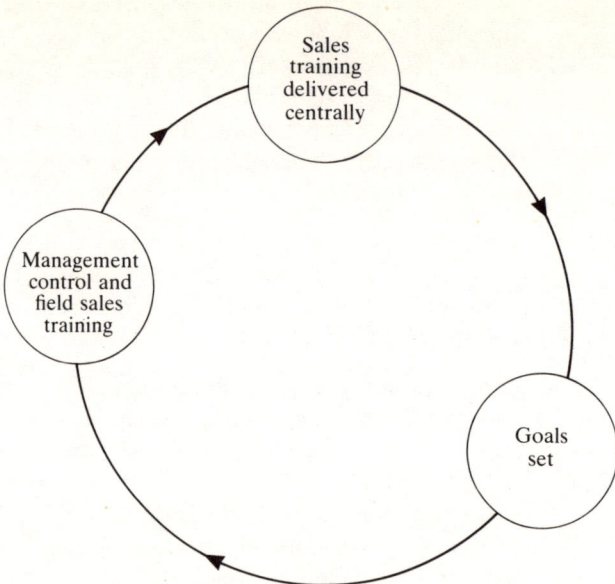

Figure 2.3   *Effective sales training*

had a strong training background and only moved into personnel in the first place because that was where the power was perceived to lie. There are as many arguments for personnel departments reporting to training managers as vice versa, but I have yet to encounter a UK company where this is so. Personnel departments have a tendency to retain the staff development function and sometimes combine it with the mystique of manpower planning. Without this their working days would certainly be less stimulating.

Personnel and training can work together, and there are obviously examples in various companies where this is the case, but it cannot be an easy relationship. One of the greatest problems associated with both departments is the untested professional, and their proliferation is more likely in personnel than in training departments. This book is not about personnel departments but I do believe that sales training departments must be staffed by salespeople. With that as proviso, sales trainers reporting to line managers who are themselves not salespeople or have not been in sales management will end in tears unless the sales trainer is given complete freedom to develop and control the sales training programme without interference. Much of this may be beyond your control. It hardly seems likely that personnel departments who have control of sales training functions will release them to enjoy equal status.

Basically, you have to accept your limits and work within the confines of what is possible. In many ways it probably makes more sense for sales trainers to work directly for the sales director or the national sales manager, as is the case in many successful salesforces in America. Sales training has a greater affinity with sales management than with personnel work. As we progress through this book and I explain the need for sales managers to accept responsibility for sales training, this structure looks even more pragmatic.

Check-list

Here is a check-list for determining at which level your training department is currently operating.

1 The department copes with all training needs, which are identified as part of the yearly staff appraisal system.
AGREE/DISAGREE
2 Considerable levels of training are provided for by external consultants.
AGREE/DISAGREE
3 The department runs a training course most weeks of the year.
AGREE/DISAGREE
4 Evaluations of internally run courses are carried out immediately after each training event.
AGREE/DISAGREE
5 Trainers are not involved in running the business.
AGREE/DISAGREE
6 The department will spend more this year than it did last year.
AGREE/DISAGREE
7 Sales training of all salespeople is the responsibility of the sales training department.
AGREE/DISAGREE
8 It is the operational managers' job to run the business, and the training department's job to make sure that all staff are trained to meet the demands of the business managers.
AGREE/DISAGREE
9 Line managers have enough to do without involving them in every bit of training that their subordinates receive.
AGREE/DISAGREE
10 You do not need to be able to sell to teach others how to sell.
AGREE/DISAGREE

Give yourself one point for each time you disagreed. If you scored between 0 and 5 you are still at Level Three. If you scored between 6 and 8 you are already at Level Two. If you scored 10 you should write a book!

Key points

1 The decision should be taken on what sort of training department you want to work in. It is a difficult choice to make because many of you will not have any power or influence. A measure of your successful transition to Level One training will be when you are asked to contribute to the company's business plan. Level One is an internal training consultancy where trainers are seen and heard. The alternative choices are a Level Three training department that acts as a clearing

house for other people's courses, or a Level Two department which is so busy delivering courses that it fails to recognize change or keep in touch with the organization's business objectives.

2 Training, and especially sales training, is a continuous process. There is no training gap between central sales courses and field training. The latter is a responsibility of the line manager who must be involved in the training process at all times. In this way Level One trainers are able to prove the effectiveness of their sales training.

3 Training is a relatively new function and as such is probably going through the growing pains of self-assertion. At present most training departments suffer from non-involvement in business decision-making processes and are viewed as a cost rather than an investment.

4 Sales people are the life blood of all sales organizations. Salespeople are not born—they are trained. Sales trainers, therefore, have a vital role to play in ensuring the company's growth and potential prosperity.

5 The practice of sales trainers reporting to personnel functions can be inappropriate.

3 Deciding on a policy and selling it

This chapter aims to answer these questions:

- What involvement is required of top management?
- How do you put together a training policy statement?
- How important is the image of the sales training department and how would you go about selling it to the rest of the company?

The MD's mission and vision

If you are putting together a sales training department for the whole organization then the only way to reach Level One is to negotiate with the person at the top. It could be that you work in a division of the company or in a subsidiary company. Whichever it is, you have to go to the person at the top and find out what they want.

This is not as easy as it sounds. In many companies training is a function that tends to do as it is told, and appears a reasonably simple process to most of those not involved in it. Top management decide what is to be done and training does something or other with the staff.

If you are any good, you know that this is not the case, and that if your sales training is to be delivered professionally and more importantly be effective, then you need the involvement of the people at the top.

Before writing your training policy statement you have to know the shape of the company to come. Where is the company set to be in twelve months time? Where will the company be in three years time? What will the company look like in five years time? The only person able to tell you this should be the person at the top.

It is surprising how many sales training departments are delivering programmes without any idea whether the training is contributing to long-term plans. In any event, your purpose here is to convince top management that sales training is a continuous process and that many managers in the company will have to change their methods of operation and perception of the training function. In order to do this you need the support of the person at the top. You should not underestimate the resistance you could encounter with some of the basic proposals in this book from operations managers who see trainers as people who should be seen and not heard. Unless you have top level backing, your well-laid plans could end up on the shelf with a host of other previous training manuals. The skeletons of corporate training failures line the many shelves of Britain's offices. Do not let yours be one of them.

Your discussion with the managing director could take the following format:

Trainer	Thank you for seeing me. I wanted to see you to talk briefly about my proposals for a new kind of training department. It will not be the sort that is constantly coming to you for more money but one that makes sales training really work.
MD	Well, that sound interesting. Most people are looking for more funding.
Trainer	I know. That's why I knew you would be interested in hearing what I've got to say.
MD	Go on.
Trainer	My impression of you is that you want things to be done effectively and professionally. I also believe that if everyone in the company was as concerned with cutting costs and increasing income as you are you would be quite pleased.
MD	I would be more than pleased; I'd be amazed.
Trainer	I firmly believe that we have to introduce a system of sales training that gets away from the course mentality. A system that integrates sales training as a vital part of a sales manager's job. In this way I believe that we can deliver ten times the current amount of training at no additional cost.

Even if you only get the impression that the chief executive is showing a passing interest in your strategy you will already be a step forward in the right direction. The crux of this strategy is that the person at the top has to believe in training. They have to believe that sales training should be continuous, and the only way to make it continuous is to concede that one of the main functions of managers is to train and develop their staff.

Some managers will resist this premise and say that training and development is the training department's job. They feel a manager's job is to deal with the important decisions and control the sales force. This is why is it important to find out where the top man stands. Without his agreement you stand no chance of working at Level One.

I believe that a manager's main function is to *develop* staff. Any fool can introduce systems which *control* staff, and a computer will do the jobs of forecasting, budgetary control and reporting. Far too many sales managers hide in offices, believing that the mundane job of training staff is for someone else while managers tackle the vital problems besetting the company. If it is believed that training is too lowly a task for managers to do then it would be better if it were not done at all.

My research has shown that sales training which does not require the manager to be totally involved and follow up in the field can be positively damaging to sales force health.

Having gained top management's blessing, there are two further things you need. One is the involvement of the chief executive in any new-style training events you schedule, and a mission statement. The involvement of the chief executive need only consist of turning up on the odd course that is run centrally, or asking specific questions of managers about their own training involvement. The mission statement is needed for you to pull the training policy statement and the training plans together. Whatever you do will be related to the mission statement. If your company has no clear statement of why it is in business, this may be your opportunity to develop one.

In any profit-making organization the inclusion in its corporate statement and your training policy statement of the words 'profit' or 'profitable' seems reasonable, but organizations are not just in the business of making profits. If this were the case then most companies would have long since sold up and invested the proceeds in order to obtain a higher return. Using the mission statement as a base will allow you to develop your training policy statement.

A training policy

The publishing of a policy statement is an important step for any sales training department. You need to take time to develop a short sentence or two that encapsulates what you are attempting to achieve. Once this policy is ratified by the managing director it gives you enormous scope to develop your training plan and get down to some serious Level One training instead of just being a 'course booker'.

Try using the mind-map system, or spidergram as it is sometimes known (see Figure 3.1). Put the words 'training policy' in the middle of a piece of paper and, spreading outwards, begin to brainstorm connected thoughts. It will not be too long before you have the bones of your statement. For example, if the company is a profit-making organization it is a good idea to refer to profit (your policy statement could include the words 'to achieve company goals profitably'). Perhaps you are also a company that is going for quality rather than volume, in which case you might say 'to achieve quality business profitably'. Taking this a stage further, the beginning of the statement could say 'The company believes that sales training is a vital ingredient in the achievement of profitable quality business'. You may also wish to state that selling is about people, both salespeople and customers, and say 'The company believes that the strength of the business is in its people and that sales training is a vital ingredient in helping our salespeople to achieve its corporate goals profitably while maintaining a high standard of quality customer service'. It will take you a few attempts to get this together and you must show the managing director your draft version. It is only draft because the MD has not had the opportunity to alter any of it or to add a word or two that will give the MD ownership. It also allows

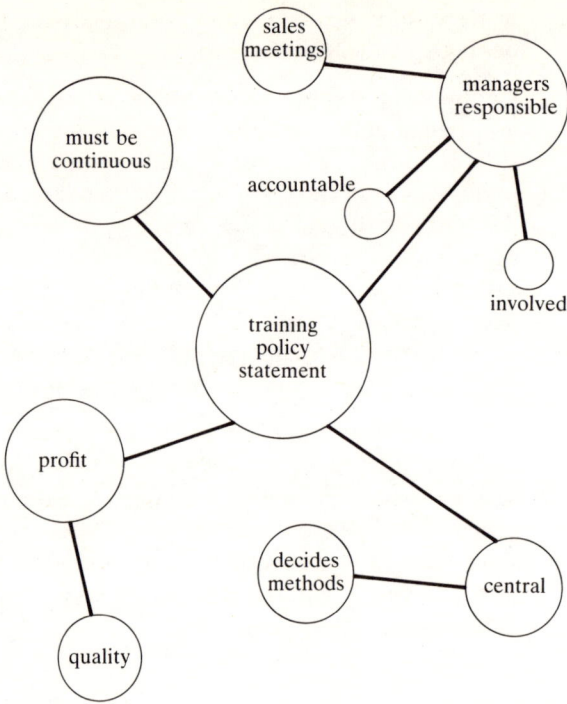

Figure 3.1 *Developing a training policy*

you to say to any Doubting Thomas manager, 'Well, this is what the boss wants, and at the end of the day we all have to do what the boss wants, don't we?'

Behind the statement, you will have a brief explanation of how the policy will work. Let's take the policy statement we have just developed. Again using the mind-mapping method you could develop some connecting words and phrases that will help to explain how the policy will work in practice. These might be:

- Sales training is continuous. We recognize that people learn skills through repetition and therefore all regional sales meetings will contain some sales training content.
- All new entrants to the sales team will be given a central form of sales training before starting their jobs, and this includes clerical staff.
- Managers are responsible for training their salespeople after this initial central training.
- All training needs will be identified by line managers.
- The sales training manager will decide the most appropriate method of satisfying those training needs.
- Central sales trainers will train managers and provide them with the tools to train their staff.
- Training is a long-term investment.

If you can get agreement on these points or on something similar which is relevant to your company, you will have taken the first steps in a long journey towards excellence in sales training.

Personal image

The next stage is to examine the sales training department's image and to begin the process of selling your policy to the rest of the firm. You may have the top person's blessing but senior executives will not go out of their way to impose your training policies or plans. The how, where and when are for you to decide, and this could be a critical period for you. A lesser mortal would balk at the task ahead, but Level One trainers are made of sterner stuff.

You should now prepare the way in which you intend to sell your ideas and the best way is to practise what you preach. You must have the right image and your own management style must be an example to the rest of the company. If you are promoting managerial involvement in training you must be seen to be involved in the training of your own staff. (If it is not your natural style, you could get away with faking it for a while, but you are bound to get found out eventually if you do.)

There is no hiding place in a Level One training department. It is not a place where failed executives can quietly disappear nor the penultimate place of employment before retirement beckons. To operate the department successfully you need to be fully committed to the task and realize that the way ahead is likely to be considerably stormy.

I will refer in more detail later to the type of people to surround yourself with but they too will need vision, stamina and a desire to succeed. If, like me, you feel that sales training is probably the most exciting and exhilarating job that anyone could have, then it is important that the team working beside you displays a similar enthusiasm and passion for the job.

Your management style needs to be one that encourages the people working for you to believe they are involved in something that will benefit them and the organization. You must stretch them to the limits of their talents, constantly moving the goalposts so that they have to push that little bit harder. And all the time you are encouraging their performance and the quality of their work, reminding them of the ultimate goal and the sense of achievement at a job excellently done. The trick is that the job will never be done. Companies that are any good never stand still and neither do good sales training departments. If anything, a good sales trainer spots when things have to change before the rest of the managers do and is already planning strategies accordingly. A good sales trainer constantly carries out 'what if?' analyses and is prepared to embrace change when needed. This is the philosophy you must engender in your team, encouraging them to take risks and to question current thinking.

You should regularly review with your team where they are in relation to the objectives that have been agreed upon individually and as a group. Even if the company has a yearly appraisal system you must introduce a bi-monthly informal appraisal or review system. Collect examples of your team's work and praise the quality of it, not the quantity. Any basic sales management training will tell you that as a sales manager it is important to concentrate on performance and results and not on activity. Concentrating on activity is for those who are not doing well and is a precursor to discipline. The only thing that matters is results. For trainers, however, what should matter is the quality and effectiveness of the training. The two go together.

Praise is important. Research has shown that salespeople need more praise than most of them currently get from managers. Managers need to praise salespeople more, you need to praise salespeople more, and you need to praise your staff when they are doing well. Sometimes it is worth praising them when they are not doing so well. At times, praise out of place can spur people on to improved performance. I recall a management trainer talking about the importance of praising salespeople. He said: 'Whatever you do, find something good to say about the salesperson's performance. I went on a field visit with a salesman the other day, and it was atrocious. The presentation was abysmal, we lost the business, and the salesman looked a mess. My natural feeling was to dismiss him on the spot, but I bit my lip and said—John, can I just say, that the way you carried that briefcase into the office, arm straight down, confident, in tune with your body, well, it was amazing, well done.' The trainer then went on to coach John about his problems and gave him the opportunity to improve. While this anecdote is exaggerated, the meaning is nevertheless valid. People listen when they are being praised, even if they know it is unwarranted. If you start with criticism people's natural instinct is to feel hurt and switch off. You know it works that way with children, and it works that way with adults.

Treat your own people as though you were a sales manager with performance targets and an eye on the bottom line. Ask them to justify what they spend by examining what they got in return and how it helps to reduce cost or increase income. Encourage them to sell their ideas to you and reward them for exceptional performance. Reward does not need to be in money. People appreciate being recognized and thanked for performance.

Adopt these and other good sales management principles and the trainers working with you will start the process of selling your message. Practise what you preach.

Production image

As mentioned earlier, you should be aiming to produce most if not all the training for your company internally. This may take a long time nevertheless, you should set about planning how to do it.

The same goes for the material you produce. It is no good asking the rest of the company to pull in their belts and look at costs and then spend a fortune employing external printers and production companies to provide your materials for you. Obviously, some common sense needs to be used. If you have to set up a studio costing a quarter of a million pounds in order to make your own videos when you could buy five years' production for the same money, then it just does not add up. On the other hand, perhaps having your own studio would mean such a reduction in the unit cost that you could expand what you may believe is a vital part of your company's method of training its salespeople.

In each case you must carry out a cost-benefit analysis together with an appraisal of what contribution to profits your proposal will make. Do not be put off by the finance department's wishes to see a quick return. Remember that you have already had the agreement that training is a long-term investment. This agreement is one of the principle elements in your policy statement and this is one of the reasons why it is there.

There are some things that you can do quite reasonably that will professionally enhance the image of your department.

Desk top publishing (DTP)

The policy of your department must be to produce material and deliver training that has an air of excellence about it. One of the best ways of producing top-class material that will boost your image is to use the facilities of desk top publishing.

Desk top publishing has revolutionized the newspaper industry and it could do the same for your department. The difference between ordinary typed material and the quality of a good desk top publishing system is the same as the difference between black and white television and colour television. No matter what the size of your training department, DTP is a must. If you have not yet invested, you will need to get some professional advice. But be warned—it will take a long time learning how best to use it and, for anyone new to computers, even with word-processing experience, DTP takes some learning. The eventual returns, however, are worth the early pain.

Once your DTP system is installed you can begin the process of selling what you do by showing what you can produce for others. Initially, this may mean just publishing course schedules, or information posters. People will notice the quality. Try writing a report and DTP it. Make certain that all the material coming out of your department is different from the material coming out of other departments. Upgrade your word-processing software so that it interacts with the DTP system and add additional font styles to the word processor so that even inter-office memos look different. Better still, if you know that the man at the top is giving a presentation, offer to help. Offer to publish anything the boss needs for a meeting—anything to get him to see what you can do. It won't be long before you start getting requests from all quarters to produce material.

A good DTP system will allow you to make highly professional hand-outs, workbooks, training manuals, and even overhead projector slides. Depending on your budget you could add a simple graphics prog-ramme that will allow you to produce graphs and charts of all kinds. You can also bolt on a 35mm slide-making capacity and go the whole hog and introduce colour printing. It may all take some time but it will be worth it. Five years ago I was quoted £35 to have a colour slide made by an outside agency and even now they can cost you up to £25 each, depending on the complexity. For a minimal outlay on equipment you can produce your own.

Time is usually the problem but, given the right environment, your staff will invest their own time to be able to learn how to produce quality material and to have total flexibility to change, upgrade and scrap material as they please without the worry of cost. I see a great many trainers using worn-out, out-of-date or badly copied material, simply because they cannot afford to replace it. There is nothing more off-putting than a trainer using poor material. Once again a marketing department would not dream of sending our poor-quality material to customers—your job is to market your department as effectively as you know how.

Films

If you are still using 18mm films and a rickety old projector it would be better to give them to a charity shop for all the good they are doing. As with all technology, unless you match the standards that people are used to at home then your message will not get across. Your company insists on its salespeople being up-to-date and using the latest methodologies to sell the company's services and products. Sales training has to be sold to salespeople. Most of them have closed minds about change and the need to improve skills and will use any excuse not to bother to update them. The use of an old projector and out-of-date films provides salespeople with an excuse for not paying attention.

Whatever you do, if you are going to show films during your training events or provide a library of films for self-study purposes then make sure you use video tape equipment. This may mean changing over to video-tape. There can be no excuse for not using the modern technol-ogy available. If you cannot afford to buy the equipment then rent it.

Generally, I would advise you to stay away from the laugh-a-minute sales training films. They are great fun and everyone enjoys them. I am certain that those who make the films enjoy them too—and are probably laughing all the way to the bank. Selling is a serious business and, while I am not against humour, I cannot see the point in many of the current sales training videos/films on the market. They debase what is an hon-ourable profession. During the long training that doctors get, I'm sure they are not shown *Carry on, Doctor* to teach them how to adopt a bed-side manner, and I doubt whether solicitors would get much out of watching a few episodes of *Porridge*. Why then do we show salespeople endless reels of comic situations? If it is to teach them how to sell—forget it.

However, there are times when a break is called for and there are a number of short videos on the market, lasting probably no more than ten minutes, which can be used to lighten a training event. Humour is an important element of any successful sales trainer's repertoire and is a prerequisite for all courses dealing with interpersonal relationships and identifying weaknesses in individual communication styles.

Choose videos that treat the subject seriously and ones that are relevant to your business. It is pointless showing a video on how to sell gardening equipment if your company sells double glazing. If you cannot find a relevant video then either have one made or do without. Whatever you do, do not try to make your own. Leave the making of videos to professionals. No matter how much technology has progressed, so that we can all now make amateur videos, they remain amateur productions.

Publications

Consider producing a regular training magazine or circular, with articles which include help and advice on current issues relevant to your company. Start to promote the professionalism of your department by showing people that you and your staff are tackling issues which are important to them. Get other senior managers involved in writing articles for the magazine, giving their viewpoints, and act as a clearing house for people's ideas and opinions. Encourage people to suggest topics you could tackle.

Try to get something published in a trade magazine which you can then circulate. Do anything, provided it is legal, to get your name and those of the people who work with you into print. There is an old Hollywood maxim that any publicity is good publicity.

Qualifications

For credibility's sake you must encourage your people to gain some professional qualifications if they don't have them already. For those that do—publicize the fact. When you produce course notes and prospectuses make certain that the qualifications of your trainers are highlighted. Professional qualifications are not a requisite for training excellence, but they certainly do no harm. They also show that you have people in your department who can compete with the best at any level.

I must emphasize that your department must act as a role model for the others. You must be seen as embodying all the qualities and attributes you are seeking to develop in others.

Never allow your own people to stop learning. If you stop learning you stop living. The vast majority of salespeople I have met stopped living a long time ago. A sales trainer's job is to revive those people and get them to open their minds and start learning again.

Encourage your trainers to keep on learning. Discourage the use of external training courses in your organization but keep in touch by getting your trainers to attend them. Sometimes they will notice material which they can adapt and use. At other times it may just reinforce what a good department you have created and how far ahead of the game you are. In this case it will increase the confidence of your own team and perhaps even convince them that you are not completely mad after all.

Trainers as consultants

As soon as you can, and when you feel confident about the team's abilities, change the job title of your staff to that of training consultant. It may be cosmetic but it will help you to sell what it is you want them to do and how you wish them to be viewed. The only way in which sales training is going to be effective is for your trainers to spend a lot more time with sales managers and a lot less time with the sales team. In the early days they might have to do some of the work for the sales manager but your long-term aim has to be to act as trainers and consultants to the managers.

Time

This image building will all take time. It is, however, part of your strategy and will be included as a major objective in your five-year training plan. Always produce a training plan and update it every six months. In this way you can show that you are concerned with the future, not the past or the present. You will deal with the present and your feet must be shown to be planted very firmly on the ground, but show that you have plans for the future that are compatible with the business.

Every six months check with senior management that your training plans coincide with how they see the business going. Tell them of the long-term nature of developing people and how your early involvement in strategic planning will help them to achieve their aims. By being aware and showing that you are concerned with the company's progress and, more importantly, are actively contributing, you will enhance your personal image and also that of the whole sales training department.

Never resist change, and never say 'No'. Better to say 'I need some time to think this thing through so that I can contribute more effectively to your plans'. If you later have to dig your heels in you will be able to do so having weighed up the pros and cons first. In some instances you will have to give way. You may have to compromise some short-term ideals but not your long-term ambitions for yourself or the department.

Spell out clearly to your people at every opportunity what your vision and goals are and be certain that theirs are the same. If someone does not pull their weight and they are going to hold you back or compromise the image you are seeking to portray, you must get rid of them quickly. If you can save them and put them in an administrative role away from other people then that is up to you. Insofar as front-line trainers are concerned, though, make sure they are good and fight tooth and nail to have them well rewarded. If you pay peanuts you will get monkeys. Make no mistake about it, the sales training function of a company is the single most vibrant and important area of the business.

This is the engine of the business and the only area of any company that is totally concerned with getting the best out of salespeople. Every other function of the company lives off salespeople's backs. You are the one who helps them to stand up in the first place.

A training plan

The publication of a training plan is an important element in selling your department. Normally, the plan would cover a three to five year period with specific detail relating to the coming year. By publishing the plan, and regularly updating it you will demonstrate the long-term nature of sales training and the company's commitment to it. It should contain the following elements:

1 **A summary** The first part of your plan should contain the major conclusions reached and a summary of the purpose and scope of the plan. No matter what else the plan contains, this is the single most important section. The chances are that this will be the only part most people will read, if they read any at all. The chief executive will also probably read the section on expenditure, but for the most part the bulk of your material will go unread. So what's the point? The point is that you do it and are seen to be doing it. The point is that you can do it and in any case it should be done. I see a significant number of companies where no such plan exists. Unless you carry out this process you will be in danger of being swallowed up by another department with a perceived high level of efficiency, or closed down altogether. The summary draws the other sections together, and is the source for discussions and presentations to other managers across the company.

2 **Mission statements and corporate aims** Within this section you publish your training policy and your mission statement. By reiterating the company's mission statement you can demonstrate how your department intends to contribute to the company's overall objectives. Sometimes it is also a reminder to everyone what the corporate aims of the company are, for many will not know. It is here that you outline the period covered by the plan and its continuous nature. This gives you the chance to display the long-term nature of the training programme and comment on the need to look at training as an integral part of the company's long-term strategies for achieving corporate success.

3 **Evaluations** It is important that you are seen to set yourself objectives that can be measured as well as outlining in detail how training intends to add value to the company's profit needs. Unless you can show that the company will get a return on its investment in training, you will always be susceptible to budgetary cut-backs. And if you do not deliver as promised? The government of the day never delivers what it promises either. The vast majority of analysts get it wrong every year, and they are supposed to be experts. The thing is to try. It will also terrify those other functional departments that never evaluate what they contribute. Your aim is to help people understand that training is not a cost, it is an investment. Like any investment, the

company is entitled to a return that at least matches a rate they could expect if the money was invested on the money market.

4 **Training schedules**   Even if you are trying to move away from running endless courses and on to providing a training consultancy, there will always be some events that you have to run centrally. In fact, in the early days, you may have to trade Level One for Level Two while you establish yourself. In the next chapter I will discuss whether training is appropriate at all in certain circumstances. Whatever the case, you may still have to react to training demands with courses until such time as you establish your credibility. In the early days, unless you have a schedule that looks busy, people will assume that you are not doing very much. Training departments are all about running courses, aren't they?

5 **Investment**   Call it investment, not costs. This is where you break down the investment per event, programme, and total training process. There are as many different ways to do this as there are training plans. Even if you are not required to submit the fine detail, you should have it available for yourself. That means being aware of the total training investment such as salary costs, lost sales opportunity time, and travelling costs. Having the information to hand and producing it at the appropriate moment will do your image a power of good.

Key points

1 The development of a training policy statement should be done in conjunction with the managing director. The main premise of your policy and that of the company must be that managers are responsible for training staff. The steps necessary for creating a policy statement are:

a) Agree overall policy and direction with the MD first. Determine the shape of the company, where it is going and what sort of people with what skills and knowledge are required.

b) Encapsulate within your policy statement the major content of the MD's mission statement. If the MD has no mission statement, help to develop one before publishing yours.

c) Ensure that your policies focus on people and the importance of investment in people if the company is to succeed.

d) If your company is a profit-making organization include the word 'profit' or a derivative in your statement. Make certain that people know that you intend to achieve results from training.

e) Publish the level of management involvement and explain in detail what people can expect from managers in terms of personal training and development.

2 After agreeing the policy and how it will apply in practical terms to your company, you should ensure that your own department is seen as a role model of professional training and management processes. The image you and your department portray is of paramount importance to the success of your overall training programmes. It should not be a case of 'do as I say, not as I do'.

3 Publish your policies and mission statements as part of an overall training plan. The training plan will be the flagship of your aims and will show your peers and boss that you have arrived and have something to contribute.
4 All material and productions coming from your department must be of the highest quality and content.
5 Encourage your staff to obtain professional qualifications and to undertake research that is relevant to the department and will enhance the training you produce.

Recommended reading

Robinson, K.R. *A Handbook of Training Management*, Kogan Page 1981.
Taylor, B. and G. Lippitt (eds) *Management Development and Training Handbook*, McGraw-Hill 1983.

4 Carrying out a training needs analysis

This chapter attempts to answer the following questions:

- What is the influence of recruitment and selection on the sales training process?
- What types of sales roles are there, and is it necessary to have a different training system for each?
- What skills, knowledge and attitude training will have to be delivered?

In many organizations the process of identifying training needs appears on the surface to be an uncomplicated if lengthy affair. I believe that identifying training needs is far from easy and needs special attention. There is a lot more to it than simply examining job descriptions—perhaps the job description is wrong in the first place. Some of the material in this chapter may not at first glance be compatible with your perception of identifying training needs, but I encourage you to give extensive consideration to it. The concepts discussed here are important to the overall understanding needed to develop your Level One department.

Influencing the recruitment policy

Before you begin to design a training programme you need to know a number of things:

- What sort of people are being recruited as salespeople?
- Is there one sales role or several?
- Will the new recruits be experienced or will you have to start from scratch?
- Are you responsible for inputting knowledge?
- How much time and resources have you got?

These are questions that affect the recruitment process and therefore you need to be involved at an early stage. It is no good employing the wrong sort of people for the sales role and expecting you to train them to sell. If people are coming in expecting to carry out a service role and you hit them with sales training where the first element is prospecting, not only will it come as a shock to them but it won't do a great deal for the first day of your course.

I have witnessed many sales training departments struggling with groups of people who do not want to be salespeople and sales trainers going through the motions trying to train people who are already asking themselves what on earth all this sales business is about. I recall one sales training event I was running where, during the second half of the day, one of the course members suddenly sat bolt upright and declared 'Just a minute, this sounds like selling!' I don't know who was more shocked, me or them.

Is training the answer to improving performance?

Being asked to deliver sales training may stroke your ego, but it may very well not be the answer, and sometimes you have to resist the temptation to try the impossible. I know many sales trainers who believe they have the power to change people. In reality, you cannot change anyone who does not already have the desire to change, and it is impossible to teach anyone to sell who does not want to sell. You will be lucky if all your sales courses are attended by people wanting to learn how to sell. On every course there is usually at least one person who does not want to be there, does not want to be in selling, and does not want to change. Now and then I have faced a training room where the majority do not want to be there.

If someone asks you to train their staff, ask yourself why they are handing them over to you. Helping them is different. If they want to learn how to train their staff themselves then you can lend a hand. You might even do it yourself, on the clear understanding that you are coaching them to take over. That is on the proviso that the staff *want* sales training. The manager may want the staff to have sales training, but the staff themselves might not want to be salespeople. A classic example of the struggle to deliver sales training to people who do not want it can be seen in financial institutions in Britain and, in particular, America, where most research has been carried out. It has been found that many companies want to sell financial services, but can't find anyone who actually wants to do the selling. Shostack calls this 'the cult of the professional'. Selling is not seen as a profession and is therefore resisted by most people in banks and building societies. It has been found that sales training fails in these establishments because the environment is not geared to a sales culture.

Salespeople are affected by the internal environment and will quickly establish whether their sales activity will ultimately be detrimental to their career aspirations. In my research I found that people have used the sales role to advance their career prospects in other operational, administrative, or managerial roles. The time in sales was seen as a necessary evil. The knack for many was not to stay in selling too long or they would become known as a salesperson.

Sales training therefore is not simply a matter of delivering the training that is requested. You have to believe that your task is realistic. The problem may be, however, that you are the only one to adopt a realistic approach.

The chief executive of a major insurance company told me recently that he was implementing a total sales and sales management training system in the company. He had spent some time in America where he bought the intellectual rights to a revolutionary new system that would turn the whole company around and build a successful sales platform for what had been up till then a traditionally staid and bureaucratic composite insurance firm. He said he was looking for a sales trainer to drive the thing through—in three months. I smiled but managed to get away before he offered me the sort of money I would be embarrassed to refuse. There are some things that are possible and some that you just take the money for. The ones you take the money for will eventually haunt you. Being a professional sales trainer will mean saying 'no' more often than 'yes'.

The confusion over sales training is rife. Managers not experienced in the sales process will assume that sales training departments are in the miracle business and that selling is a process that any fool can learn. The selling process is easy to understand but very difficult to carry out effectively. I understand the rules of football very well but I have always played it badly. If I concentrated full-time on it, I believe I could become reasonably good—that is, if I were a lot younger. Given time most people could become reasonably good at selling, if they really wanted to, but those that do want to are in a minority. Most people in selling want the easy life; the last thing they want is to have to put up with the most prevalent factor in selling—rejection. It is not the lack of success that makes salespeople fail, it is the inability to cope with rejection.

For sales training to work, selection has to work. For selection to work, *you* have to be involved in the process. You have to be able to point out what can and cannot be achieved in terms of training non-salespeople to sell or undoing years of poor sales experience, management and training elsewhere.

You have got to be involved in the recruitment policy in order to inject some common sense into the process. Unless you do, the personnel professionals and psychologists will stitch you up and pass on some instant training disaster cases your way. If you do not have your say about the type of people that are recruited and the expectations that managers and personnel staff have about the effects of sales training, you will end up on the slippery slope to misery and ruin.

Sales roles

It could be said that there are as many sales roles as there are sales jobs. My research seems to suggest that each company has its own unique culture and fosters its own sales roles. This would explain the successful salesperson who goes to another company, perhaps in an identical field, but fails. Successful selling has a lot to do with confidence. I also believe that most buying decisions are made emotionally. Logic is used to justify emotional buying decisions. Putting these things together, it is hardly surprising that in a different environment a salesperson may well not perform as expected. Motivational theory as set out by Maslow, McGregor and Herzberg confirmed that people are affected by the organizational environment. I believe that the influence of the organizational environment on salesperson success is greatly misunderstood and underplayed.

Because selling roles vary so much, the level of sales training needed for each role differs correspondingly. Most organizations, however, tend to assume that there is only one form of sales training. They believe that it is about learning techniques such as overcoming objections and closing. In many situations this type of training does work but it is not professional selling and operates in an environment where one-off selling is the norm. My advice is directed towards forming long-term professional sales relationships with customers, although your particular sales environment may not advocate that ideal.

Nykodyn identified seven possible sales roles which are useful descriptions of the existing variety:

- a product deliverer
- an inside order taker
- an outside order taker
- a creator of goodwill, and educator of potential users
- a technical consultant
- a seller of tangibles
- a seller of intangibles

The types are self-explanatory on a simplistic level, but perhaps show the variety and complexity of sales roles available in a generic sense only. For example, a seller of tangibles could be at one end of the scale a balloon seller and at the other an armaments dealer. Surely the type of sales training used to train these two people cannot be the same? Or can it?

The preponderance of sales training agencies in the market and the variety of packages in circulation seem to indicate a huge assortment of solutions to specific sales roles and yet closer examination will reveal considerable similarities. After all, how many ways are there of asking for the order?

You should identify in some considerable detail what the sales job entails. List all the activities that are involved, together with the results expected. Sometimes this may mean expanding the job description, which in some areas may have failed to describe the sales process fully, or shows faulty understanding of what the job entails. For example, it seems pointless to list prospecting as an activity without realizing the full implications of just what prospecting is. Figure 4.1 shows the sort of process you should adopt. First, write down the word and then expand it to a full description of the activity. The dictionary defines prospecting as exploring for gold or working a mine experimentally. It means digging, and if you dig in the wrong place, or you don't know what you

Job tasks	Full explanation
Prospecting	Finding people to sell to by going through local business directories and identifying suitable companies who may be in the market for our goods.
	Composing letters which will stimulate interest and then following up with a telephone call that will gain an appointment to see a decision maker.
	Obtaining referred leads.

Figure 4.1   Training analysis

are digging for or what it looks like, then you might end up with nothing. You could waste a lot of energy and time. Sales people generally hate prospecting and will find a million and one things to do to avoid it. In most professional sales roles, however, salespeople are employed to prospect. The dictionary definition of prospecting as an activity fails to mention the resilience and energy required to carry out that function of the job. Anyone can be trained to prospect, but will they want to? At an interview, a manager may ask whether a candidate will prospect and how, but the true measure of whether they will lies not in the answer, but in the manner in which the answer is given.

Much of personal selling is to do with personality. Guion has said that not only do sales roles differ but the personality characteristics required also vary greatly. This whole area of personality and recruitment is fraught with difficulties. It also leaves sales trainers with complex tasks to perform, some of which may just not be possible. You need to ascertain whether people are being employed who can already do the job, or whether you are supposed to train them to do the job. Figures 4.2 and 4.3 give examples of processes you could develop to stimulate thinking on what is possible. In many ways personnel policies can be contradictory. On the one hand companies are seeking people who can sell, and on the other they employ sales trainers who are supposed to teach people how to sell. It could be that your job is not to teach people *how* to sell but *what* to sell. In which case, what is the outcome supposed to be?

The more the company wants you to change existing people, the more impossible the task becomes. You stand a reasonable chance of success with new entrants to the company, but even then your programme could resemble a computer operation—GIGO: garbage in, garbage out. Those people not previously employed in sales roles internally will fight tooth and nail against sales training. You might have their bodies in the training room but you will rarely have their minds.

Must be able to:	Can be trained to:
• Prospect • Persuade • Empathize with customers • Show enthusiam • Display self-motivation	• Collect information • Display product • Answer questions • Sell • Complete administration

Figure 4.2   *Recruitment or training?*

Must be able to:	Can be trained to:
• Show understanding of the total job, once explained, in particular the part referring to prospecting • Display a desire to be trained to sell better • Show a thirst for knowledge • Display a desire to win, and give examples of past achievements, not just in selling	• Sell • Show a full understanding of the product range • Use the telephone effectively • Have a greater awareness of own communication style

Figure 4.3   *Expanding the analysis of skills and attitudes*

This is why you need to be involved in the recruitment process. Your job is to help focus attention on exactly what the problem is—the fact that there are not enough salespeople in the market to satisfy the demand. This is fundamental. Recruitment processes, no matter how in-depth, no matter how technical, and no matter what personality identification procedures are involved, are no guarantee in helping you to get the right people to train.

Recruitment, assessment and selection mechanisms have a proclivity to look for the rounded person but, as Drucker says, there is no such being as the rounded person. People with high skills in one area usually have high failings in another. Recruitment processes try to find people with equal strengths across the board. In practice, this comes up with employees who have the lowest common denominator in skills. A common method is to establish what skills are required by salespeople (see Figure 4.4). The skills identified may be:

• persuasiveness
• social skills

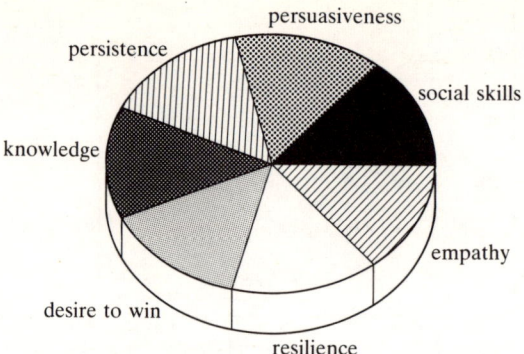

Figure 4.4 *Desired skills and attributes in a salesperson*

- desire to win
- empathy
- knowledge
- resilience
- persistence

—but how much of each, and who really knows what the mix should be? Does it matter if one skill is missing or can you train someone to be resilient or to have empathy? Some agencies say that you can and that by internal measurement it is possible to determine the ideal profile for your company. What about those people you did not employ though— the one's your selection process rejected? If you come up with the ideal profile for a salesperson, does that mean that the success of other companies is merely a figment of your imagination? If other companies are more successful than yours it might be a good idea to get their profile of the ideal salesperson rather than use your own.

The reality is probably closer to the situation shown in Figure 4.5. Further out on the edges where high skills areas are found there is a greater chance that gaps will occur in other areas. The centre is the only place where an equal spread of skills is found, but here they are of a low level.

Another problem here is that asking, for example, for highly developed social skills, presupposes that there is a clear understanding of what social skills are. In the particular market that the company operates, it might mean that the sales role involves a high-profile salesperson, someone who is outgoing, perhaps loud or dynamic. This profile may not fit with the internal environment. Internally the company might be sober or bureaucratic.

Recruiting salespeople is easy enough, providing you are not too concerned about the quality. In selling, as in buying, the argument will always be one of quantity versus quality. Poor sales managers tend to concentrate on quantity of calls rather than quality of calls. It is easier to monitor activity than quality of performance: the former can be done in the office, the latter has to be done in the field.

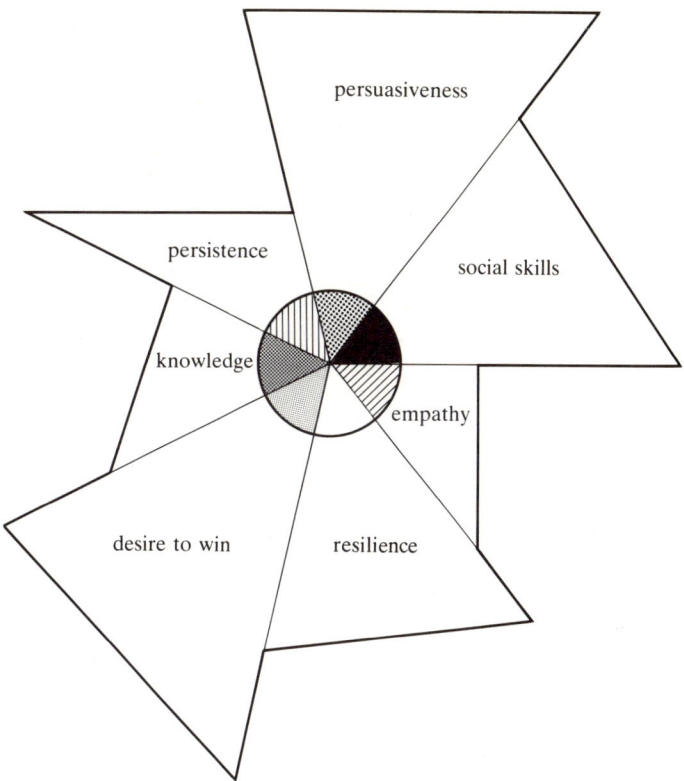

Figure 4.5 *Actual skills and attributes*

Making salespeople sell successfully, and putting together the right sales training programme is impossible unless it is recognized that the sales trainer has an important role to play in determining the company's recruitment policies. Yet, ultimately, good salespeople are virtually impossible to find. Those that are any good do not need to apply to join your company unless you are offering an astounding benefit package, in which case it will prove impossible to sort the chaff from the wheat. Those that do apply will always look better on paper than they do when they start working for you. They might be very good at the interview, but then it is not difficult to fool employers at the recruitment stage. Perhaps your own company is one of those that, in the vain hope of not making costly employment mistakes, advertises for self-motivated, enthusiastic, confident salespeople with a proven track record. Maybe you should ask yourself why—if they are all of these things—they should want to join you. It could be that they want to move because they are not very good at what they are doing somewhere else. So you take up their references, but are you sure that taking up references will help you get a good salesperson? If they were any good, no matter what it took, the company they are leaving would make certain that they at least match what you are offering rather than let them go. Think about the situation:

A   The market for quality professional salespeople is far greater than the availability of salespeople to fill it (see Figure 4.6).
B   You have a good salesperson who is dissatisfied.
C   You let him go to a competitor.

This doesn't make much sense, but it is precisely what happens every day because many companies are naive enough to think they can employ a replacement without any difficulty. This belief is reinforced by the large number of replies they receive to an employment advertisement. These companies must ask themselves why successful salespeople would want to leave their present company. In many cases the only people applying to your company for sales jobs are salespeople who have failed somewhere else. They will tell you that they are taking a drop in earnings to join you because you are a dynamic firm that is going places; they will tell you they were misunderstood in their last company; or that they have been looking for the opportunity to join an aggressive company like yours and will break every sales record in your book. But if those asking to join your company at the bottom of the sales ladder were really so successful before, why are they not earning the sort of money that you could not afford to pay them?

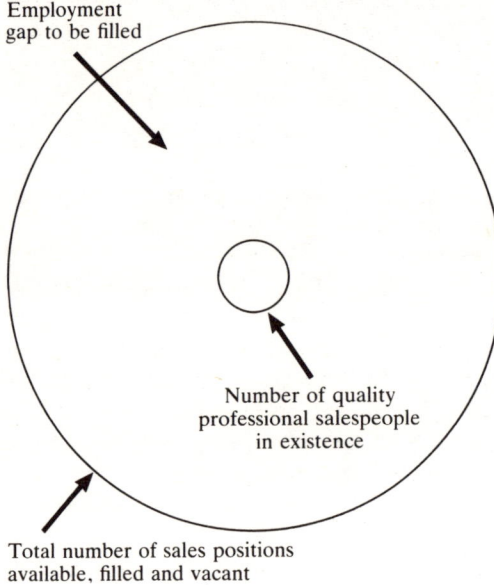

Figure 4.6   *The gap training has to fill*

There is a naive belief in some companies that all the world's good salespeople are queuing up to join them. Yet paradoxically they also devise complicated selection procedures to weed out potential failures. They will buy any process or system, no matter how expensive, just to make certain that the applicants are the best available. Then they contact the previous employer to ask for a reference. The only valid purpose for doing this is to check whether the candidate was dismissed for dishonesty. The rest will usually be either a fabrication of lies and half truths, or a confirmation that the salesperson was not much good.

Previous employers play the same game as you do. Who cares about people once they have left? If companies told the truth about former employees they would earn themselves such a bad name in the employment market that nobody would want to join them in the first place. Just because salespeople say they were successful somewhere else it does not mean they will be successful for you. Have you ever employed someone who was successful elsewhere but not for you? Or course you have.

Your company has to understand that possibly the most important function within the firm is that of sales training. No matter what the background of trainees, whether experienced or not, they have to be trained to sell for your company. And it will be less painful for you to train people to sell if they have not been in selling before. Experienced salespeople will bring with them all the bad habits and attitudes which have made them so unsuccessful in the past (Figure 4.7). There will be a few who will seize the opportunity to start again and will open their minds to change, but it will be unusual to encounter many of these. With salespeople, you are possibly dealing with the most arrogant and yet insecure set of individuals in the workforce—they think they are individuals when in reality their methods and techniques are predictable. They do the same things day in and day out. Salespeople believe that selling is about the 'gift of the gab', or learning to overcome objections, or closing technique. Once learned, that's it.

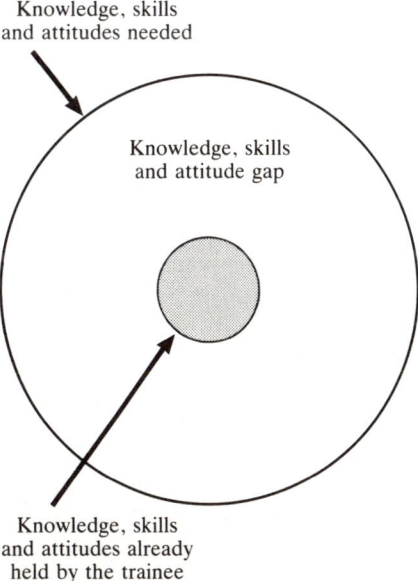

Figure 4.7 Designing a training solution

The more experienced the salesperson the harder your job will be to retrain them. That is why you need an *excellent*, not just a good, sales trainer. It also means that sales trainers have to make senior managers understand that sales training in isolation does not work.

Training salespeople requires an integrated system of training, management and motivation. A training system developed to operate in isolation is better than no training system at all, but only marginally. The best form of sales training is that which is totally involved in all the operational processes of management and is able to influence recruitment policy. The best chance your company has of sales success and long-term survival is to train your own salespeople, your own way, from scratch. Employ only those people who are prepared to relearn everything they know about selling—in many ways it is better to employ those who know nothing about selling but want to learn. New recruits with no sales experience fare far better initially than those with previous experience. After that, their long-term tenure is totally reliant upon management control, motivation and training. Salespeople with experience expect little of sales managers and have a tendency to be more resilient. Those with no experience of sales managers are quickly disillusioned by poor managers who know little of motivation and fail to deliver continuous training.

Knowledge, skills and attitude

Training salespeople involves the acquisition of knowledge, skills and attitude (see Figure 4.8). Knowledge and skills can be taught, but attitude can only be learned. By that I mean that the salespeople themselves will determine whether or not to put the knowledge and skills into practice.

Knowledge

If the acquisition of knowledge has more to do with education than training, should you therefore adopt educational principles in determining knowledge levels? Is there a difference between training and education? Perhaps there is. You wouldn't mind your daughter coming home and saying that she had received sex education at school today. You would probably blow a fuse if she said she had received sex training!

Knowledge, it is said, forms the basis of a salesperson's career. Without knowledge of the company's products, the market available, and the role of the company in that market, a salesperson may be placed at a disadvantage by customers' questions about the product, a situation that could ultimately result in missed sales opportunities. I agree with those who advocate product competency in salespeople—but a word of warning. A lot of salespeople know everything there is to know about their company's products: they have a total appreciation of where the market is, and even a clear understanding of their company's place in that market, but could not sell water to a thirsty man. Every salesforce has experts who cannot sell and I am sure that yours is the same. This is especially true of the insurance industry where legislation has encouraged those with existing product knowledge to seek more.

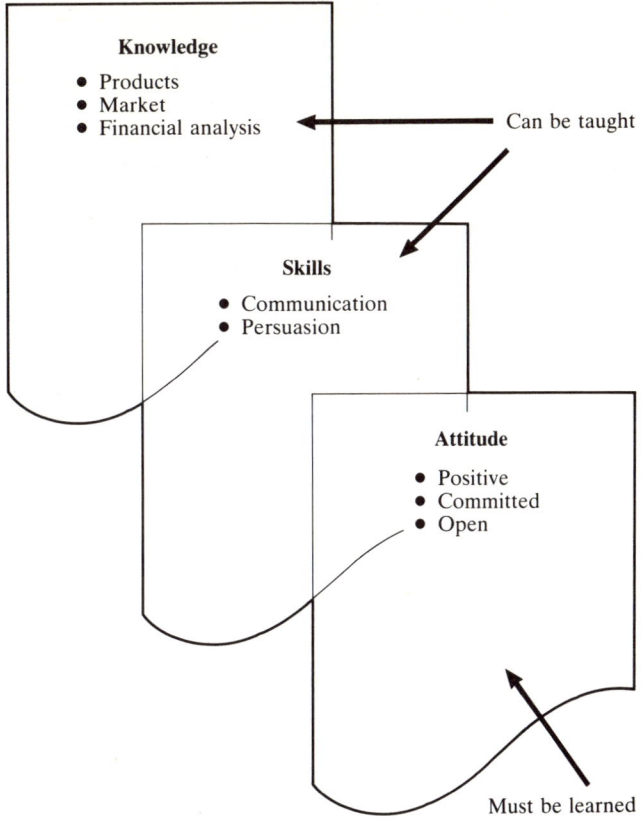

Figure 4.8 *Successful selling*

Over a seven-year period I conducted a number of surveys about training needs. Top of the list each time came the need for more product knowledge training—at least, the *perceived* need for product knowledge training. Try it some time. Ask trainees, experienced or not, what they feel they need more training in. Include these items in the list:

- Product knowledge
- Selling skills—practice
- Selling skills—theory
- Attitudes and self-awareness
- Buyer behaviour
- Company marketing policy and plans

I can guarantee that selling skills, practice and theory, will come bottom of the list and product knowledge will come top. You could be more sneaky and break product knowledge down into specific products if you like, to bulk out the list. The more products your company has, the more the perceived need will be to deliver product knowledge courses and training. There is a theory that the need for product knowledge courses increases in direct proportion to the number of product knowledge courses available. Most salespeople, except the good ones—a tiny minority—will try to avoid any environment in which they have to sell or practise their selling skills. Product knowledge training provides a safe haven for poor salespeople. In my experience there is rarely a need for product knowledge training in a company after initial training, unless you are launching a new product or service, and then it is doubtful how much is necessary. One thing is for sure, however: on the launch of a new product or service, the most popular place to be in the company is in the training department. With that in mind, I should tell you that the most unpopular place to be is the *sales* training department. After all, if you could sell you would be out selling, wouldn't you? 'Those that can sell, sell. Those that can't sell, train. Those that can't train, administrate'.

Sales trainers are hurt by these jibes and lose their confidence, so they run as many product training courses as they can to gain brownie points. Forget it. Sales training departments should not be running product knowledge courses—perhaps such courses should not be run at all. Anyone can acquire product knowledge. In some instances, however, the company may have a higher opinion of people with knowledge than they have of people with selling skills. It is part of your job to prove to them what a waste of resources it is trying to impart product knowledge to people too stupid to learn it for themselves. Worse still, it is pointless giving product knowledge to people who already have it, but want a couple of days off selling in order to get some more.

If you were to test your salespeople before running a course you would probably be surprised how much they already know. In fact, if you made periodic testing compulsory in your company, and made employment depend on it, you would be absolutely amazed how competent your salespeople would become! You could take this a stage further. Give those you are considering for employment some self-study material before you employ them, saying that their application will receive further attention once they have achieved a certain knowledge level. You might be pleasantly surprised how much people can teach themselves, and those that accept the task are probably the sort of people you want, anyway.

I agree that salespeople need product knowledge to give them additional confidence, and the more they know the more confident they should be. High levels of product knowledge, however, like high academic qualifications, are no guarantee of sales success. I found that those with qualifications and/or high competency levels in terms of product knowledge were no more or less successful than those without. Your own internal policies may dictate a need for high competency or qualifications. This is up to you, but there is no evidence to support the necessity for them.

Determine what your salespeople need to know and how they will acquire that knowledge, not for the sake of knowledge, but because it will make them more confident. It is difficult to gauge whether successful salespeople are more confident because they are successful, or successful because they are confident. A high level of product knowledge may make salespeople more confident, but confident about what? I have seen many apparently confident salespeople fall to pieces in the face of a difficult customer or at the thought of cold telephoning. Their confidence related to product knowledge and not to selling. That is the problem with the many lists produced, indicating the characteristics required by successful salespeople. They do not go into enough depth and rarely understand what makes a truly successful salesperson.

For new starters, and for new product launches, it is important to give people a grounding or foundation. After that I believe it is up to each individual to acquire further knowledge and to return to basics.

When determining what level of knowledge is necessary, include these topics in your list of training needs:

- Product features
- Selling theory
- Company politics

Product features   It matters not how you produce this material as trainees will have forgotten most of it within hours of leaving a course or of reading it. This will be true whether you desk top publish it (DTP), put it in the form of computer-based training (CBT), or write it out in longhand. At least with DTP or CBT everybody will be suitably impressed. I will refer more to CBT in a later chapter.

Selling theory   To understand the sales process people should study selling. If you are unable to put together some study material yourself, consider providing new starters with reading material which you can lend them on a library basis during their training period. No matter how many trainees you have, the costs involved in providing this type of study material will be worth it in the long run. Some of the material mentioned in this book includes case studies and tests. Or it should be a simple task for you to devise some.

It is somewhat depressing that everyone in selling seems to think they know everything about the subject of selling without having undertaken any study except in the 'university of life'. The university of life is probably one of the finest educational institutions in the world, but it takes a lifetime to study there. Lots of salespeople, sales managers and trainers consider themselves professional and yet deep down they know they are not. They have not undertaken a period of study. I know of no other profession where just turning up allows you to be called a professional. Many salespeople hide behind product knowledge as a means of justifying their professional misconception of status; they love spending all their time learning about the product.

Trainers get somewhere near the truth about product knowledge training when they say that the most important thing to learn is what a product *does*, not what it is. I believe it is far more important to find out what the product can *become* in the eyes of the customer. And that requires skill.

Company politics   Salespeople need a thorough grounding in company structure and operational details, such as who does what, and who to contact for information or to get something done. Within this section, you should teach the trainee how to survive the 'internal relationships' game (see Figure 4.9). Some salespeople fail, not because they cannot sell, but because they do not know how to play the 'internal relationships' game. I would guess that many good salespeople fail because they are willed to fail by people not committed to their success. For example, a new salesperson may have a relatively easy task selling to outsiders, but it is the 'insiders' who will determine the perceived quality of success. In some organizations it is more important to get on with the boss than it is to sell. The larger the company, the more important it is to get on with other people. The more bureaucratic the company, the less importance it attaches to selling roles and the more it believes there is a never-ending supply of salespeople. In some cases the boss's secretary has more power than the salesperson and her impression of salespeople will have more effect on their career progress than any number of orders.

Selling is an emotional business and for most new starters the number of internal relationships in a company can be daunting and fraught with danger. If your organization operates this inner sanctum mentality where being a new salesperson is like negotiating a pontoon across a piranha-filled lake, then you have two choices:

1 Change the way your company operates, especially its perception of sales—a task that might take years and kill you in the process; or
2 Let new salespeople know what the score is and how to survive it.

The better salespeople will bruise more internal relationships. You have to decide and help your company to resolve what is more important— selling, or getting on with other people in the company. If you are not sure, or the answer is both, or the latter, then you should put a marker in this page; return to the beginning of this book and read up to here again. Keep doing this until you can answer—selling. Your concern may be that you want quality selling, or you may feel that if people cannot form good relationships internally, then they will have problems forming them externally. Believe me, it is possible to be hated by every single person in the company, but be a great salesperson externally. So far as quality is concerned, be happy that they can sell first, and then work on improving the quality.

Identifying knowledge training needs is easy. Identifying the skills required is more difficult.

Skills   What are the skills that salespeople need? Can you teach these skills from scratch, or will it take too long and you will have to rely on recruiting people who already have these skills?

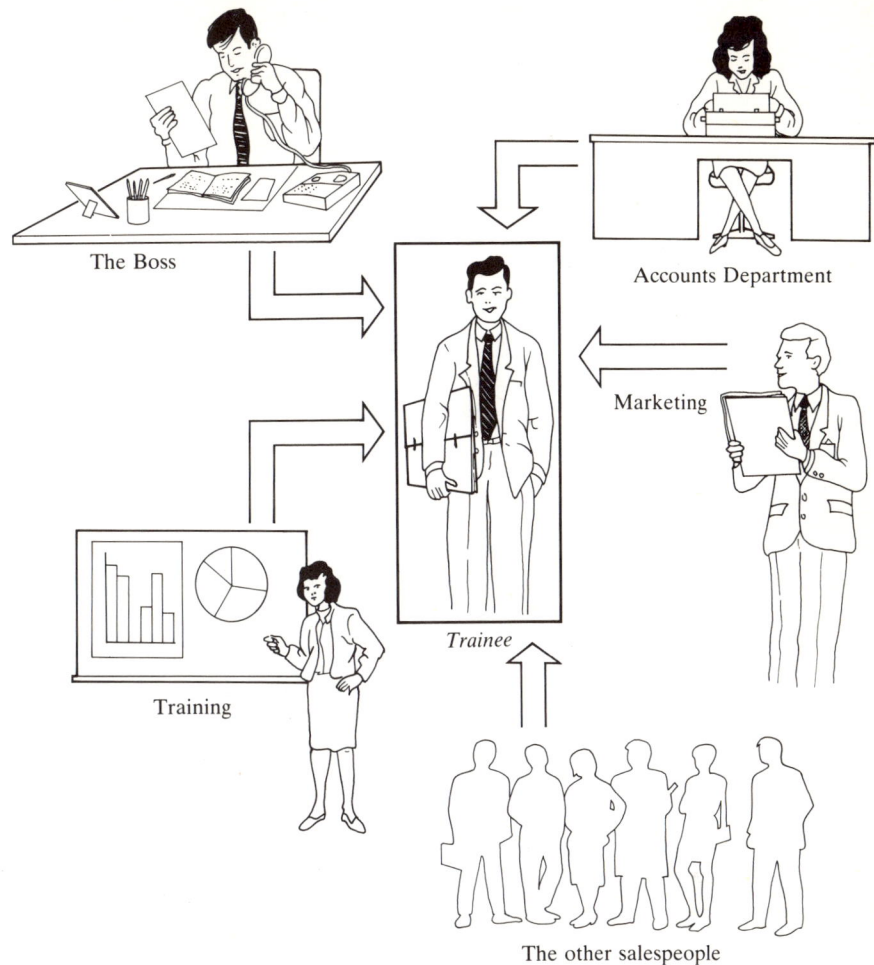

The Boss

Accounts Department

Marketing

Trainee

Training

The other salespeople

Figure 4.9 *Internal relationships in an organization*

Let us assume that your salespeople are responsible for generating their own customers and for selling to them cold. In this way we should cover the total gambit of possible sales roles. By breaking the job down you should be able to analyse in some detail the skills required. This process should also be part of the business plan. It is at this stage that you and your company will be able to determine whether the sales role is possible or not. Unless trainers are involved in this stage of the business plan, the company could blindly create roles that are either impossible to fill, or cost so much in training that the company cannot hope to make a profit out of the sales transaction.

Let us suppose that the company decides to enter a market where, in order to sell into it, salespeople have to build relationships over a long time span. The company may assume that people can be trained to sell in a shorter period than is realistically possible. The top executives may be sold a sales training package which on paper looks as if it is relatively easy to train salespeople to get past buying obstacles. On paper, and in classrooms, sales training looks an easy affair. Overcoming objections is a piece of cake, and the closing technique works every time. I can honestly say that in a classroom I can overcome any objection that trainees put to me, and can always close on a trainee and thereby get an order. I know, however, that if the vast majority of salespeople used these techniques in the field, they would get thrown out of their customers' premises. What works on courses does not necessarily work in the field.

What does work is a concentration on communication, both verbal and, more importantly, non-verbal; teaching salespeople more about themselves than about the company's products; training them to feel good about the company, its products and services, and their role in contributing to corporate goals. This takes time, but produces adaptable salespeople who can react to the uniqueness of each sales situation. Your job is to convince the MD and then others that the wait will be worth it in the long run. Is time important or do you want the training to work?

A good sales trainer will help the company set realistic business plans by saying what is possible and what is not. Yet it is rare for a trainer to become involved in the formation of business plans and strategies, and for this reason most sales training is totally non-effective. A company gets the sales training it deserves.

Prospecting

Prospecting, as I have already said, implies digging for gold. To find the gold a lot of dirt has to be moved. Prospecting is hard work and is the part of selling that most salespeople do not want to do. It is the process that involves the highest level of rejection and will ultimately determine who fails and who succeeds. Within any given sales area there is a population market, a possible target market, and an actual response market (Figure 4.10). Those who will eventually buy may be a fraction of the population market and this will be determined by the product or service you are selling and the competition, as well as the prevailing external situation such as economic climate. To get to the centre of the prospecting circle is difficult and requires determination, perseverance and willingness to encounter rejection. You might even consider including tests for these characteristics in your selection process: either role playing situations which examine these traits or asking for confirmable examples of their display in the past.

It is not sufficient to point out that salespeople have to prospect, without fully understanding what prospecting involves. Before talking to other managers about their business plans, you must understand and get them to understand what is involved in every area of the sales role. The first and last hurdle may well be prospecting. If you cannot train people to get to see customers in the first place, then no matter how

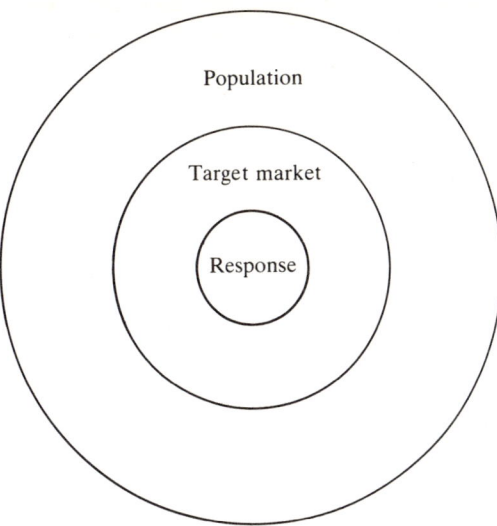

Figure 4.10 *Prospecting*

good your company's products are, no matter how competitive your package, no customer will see it.

Decide first what the 'prospecting' market looks like. If the gold is in the desert you will need a different set of tools from those required if the gold is in the mountains. You might even need a different sort of person, perhaps someone who is used to the heat. That same person may be no good to you at the top of a mountain.

Draw up a chart showing the possible sources of prospects. For example, you may be part of a larger organization with a ready-made customer database. I have seen people succeed in an environment where a customer database was available, and then fail miserably when the database was removed. The ensuing profile of the required salesperson may be different to that required if your company has no existing database to work from. Identifying the possible sources will allow you to expand that initial description into ones which may give you a greater insight into the skills required. It could also allow you to work closely with the marketing department in determining who does what, and what help can be given to whom. In this particular case direct mailing could help the salesperson to generate enquiries or even just to warm up potential customers.

From these descriptions you can ascertain what the sales processes may look like and how much prospecting the salesperson actually has to do. You should also be able to put together the initial design of possible training approaches to use.

Your next step is to isolate each job task and break it down into a comprehensive description that will allow you to gauge whether training is viable or even possible.

An example of elaborating the mere word prospecting into something more understandable could be:

In our company prospecting means finding people to sell to by going through local business directories and identifying suitable companies who may be in the market for our goods; composing letters that will stimulate interest and then following up with a telephone call that will gain an appointment to see a decision maker; also obtaining referred leads.

This looks simple enough, but what is involved? Let us examine in more detail what each part means by analysing the skills required.

Looking through business directories

Some of the skills involved could be:

- being organized and having time management disciplines;
- being able to scan material, isolating the relevant and discarding the trivial;
- analysing geographic possibilities—is the area too big to cover?
- identifying associated possibilities, such as using existing contacts to gain introductions to newly sought customers;
- determining whether the potential is too big. The company or individual may not deal on a local basis or may be part of some much larger concern.

Composing letters

Is this the salesperson's responsibility or is there a central marketing function that provides standard letters? If the salespeople have to produce anything in writing, what is their English like? What does their written work look like? Is it important?

Writing is a skill that can be learned but it could take considerable time. It is quite often the case that good salespeople are appalling administrators. You need to agree what it is the salesperson is responsible for in terms of administration and then ask why. Can you combine sales ability with complex administrative functions? If it is difficult, then consider divorcing adminstration completely from selling. Remember, internally it can be the way in which salespeople complete their administrative burden that can dictate the perception in which they are held. Managers soon tire of complaints from purchasing, finance and marketing about tardy or untidy paperwork from salespeople, and salespeople quickly become demotivated by the importance attached to it. Is it imperative that salespeople do administrative tasks, anyway? I have found that good administrators and good salespeople are rarely the same people. Part of your task may be to say that you can train people to administrate or to sell, but not both. You design systems that allow salespeople to sell and administrators to administrate. It sounds simple enough and yet thousands of salespeople are plagued by the sort of administrative burdens that could be carried out by other people more effectively, at a fraction of the cost.

Telephoning prospects

Will these be service calls or will they be cold-canvassing calls? The salesperson you are dealing with may be a terrific face-to-face presenter, but could fall to pieces on the telephone. Will your salespeople be telephoning people at work or at home? What do they sound like on the telephone? What should they sound like? Are they selling a product or service, or are they attempting to get appointments? Do your own salespeople have to use the telephone or are you able to organize a telemarketing operation to do it for them?

I have seen some salespeople fail, not because they couldn't sell, but because they were afraid to pick up the telephone. This could be a cause of poor performance which is not spotted, unless you stay close to what is happening day by day in the operation. In many salesforces where the emphasis is on activity and not results, it can be the small performances that go unnoticed. Picking the telephone up seems a reasonably minor thing to do. In the eyes of some salespeople, it is everything. Sales managers who concentrate on activity get activity; those who concentrate on results get results. By concentrating on activity, areas of performance like telephoning can give misleading results. It is commonplace for performance to increase on field visits by managers, and usually that performance is an act. Many salespeople have a real fear of using the telephone to canvass, where the chance of rejection is ten times greater than face-to-face canvassing. As a sales trainer you must recognize that salespeople surround themselves with a protective shell that says 'Telephoning—a piece of cake' whereas, in reality, they may only force themselves to make telephone calls when the manager is present or they are desperate for business. Don't underestimate the amount of time you will have to spend on telephone sales technique if it is a necessary part of the job.

In the market in which you are operating, is it easy to get to a decision maker or will the salesperson need considerable levels of skill in order to get through?

This is a significant area of potential failure for salespeople and you need to take extreme care when analysing the skills required.

Referred leads

The greatest source of future business comes from those people already buying. Most people buy on recommendation from others who have already bought. But, while it is relatively easy to train people how to do it in the classroom, getting them to ask regularly for referred leads in the field is difficult. Is it, therefore, necessary for the salespeople to get referred leads or could they survive without them? What is involved in asking for referred leads? Is it timing or is it just a case of asking every time? In most cases it is a matter of attitude.

Attitude

It is possible, with enough time and resources, to give people all the knowledge required for the job, and have them learn all the necessary skills, but unless they have the right attitude to use that knowledge and practise those skills then your training will have been a waste of time.

Defining the right attitude is a complex issue. We hear a lot about having a positive mental attitude in sales training and I would go along with the theory that positive people will tend to be more successful at selling than negative people. It does, however, remain a theory. I've met plenty of miserable salespeople who appear to be successful, but I do believe that attitude counts more than either knowledge or skills in isolation. A person with the right attitude will succeed in any case, but having both knowledge and skills will rarely work without the right attitude. But attitude has sometimes been confused with behaviour and *displaying* a positive attitude could perhaps be just as effective as having one.

The school of thought expressed by Chrissy says that behavioural training should be a requisite for all salespeople. On the other hand, Rae says that you cannot hope to change people's behaviour—the best you can do is to make people more aware of the effect their behaviour has on other people. Similarly, it is said that attitude is impossible to change and therefore you should test for the right attitude, whatever that is, at the recruitment stage.

I find that each sales situation is unique in the same way that each communication event between two or more people is different. Each sales situation demands a different approach; salespeople have to remain flexible in their approach and trainers need to look for ways to teach that flexibility. Perhaps this also demands that salespeople need the sort of attitude that makes them want to learn more about their current attitudes and the way in which their behaviour affects others. Unfortunately, this desire to open the Pandora's box rarely exists. While salespeople are narcissistic and interested in examining their personality characteristics, they soon become sceptical when adverse feedback is given, and seldom want to examine or have others observe their negative behaviour. I once gave a trainee honest feedback about his behaviour and he said: 'My behaviour has made me very successful in the past, and will continue to make me successful in the future. Are you suggesting that I will fail?' Of course, I said no. 'However, if I were to show that by modifying your behaviour you will be ten per cent more successful than you have been in the past, that would be helpful, wouldn't it?' He agreed. The tragedy of it was that he failed to recognize a sale in my question and his agreement, subsequently failed to seize the opportunity to learn new skills, and ultimately failed in the job.

It is possible to change attitude and behaviour. Festinger showed that by changing behaviour, attitude changes were also possible. Obviously it takes a long time, but then so does learning any new skill or changing firmly held beliefs. Attitude is made up of beliefs that are formed by past experiences. We are who we are, believe what we believe, and have the attitudes we have, because of what happened to us in the past.

But it does not need to remain that way. Festinger says that by changing behaviour a cognitive dissonance is created which is only relieved by changing attitudes to suit the new behaviour.

I like the story about Mark Twain, who said that when he was sixteen he was dismayed by his father whom he reasoned to be probably the stupidest man in the world. Later he said, 'By the time I became twenty-one I was amazed how much my father had learned'.

The effect that a sales trainer can have on attitude is a difficult one to gauge. It has been said that trainers themselves have no effect at all, and that people learn best through interactive events such as discussion groups or case study work. I think this is true of some trainers. I also know from experience that a really excellent sales trainer can help to change attitude—for a while. It might last only for a day, or an hour. But that hour may just be enough to make someone want to do something about changing instead of just thinking about doing something. For sales trainers to be successful in developing the right attitude, they need trainees who have already decided—perhaps not totally—that it is time they did something different, and that is all you can hope for. Salespeople are not stupid. They know who's to blame for poor performance. It's whether you catch them early enough before they repeat the same old mistakes. One problem with training new starters is that they sometimes lull themselves into a false sense of security, believing that the change of company alone will guarantee success, when really the change that is needed is in themselves. A really good sales trainer, given enough time initially, will help people to understand where change is most needed, and how important attitude is.

Attitude is all-powerful. It determines our behaviour and, effectively, will determine our success or failure in any particular venture. Spotting the right attitude is a difficult and some would say impossible task. Research has shown that the greatest problem we have as human beings when observing others is to correctly align behaviour with attitude and that spotting either is no predictor of the other. People who display a positive attitude are not necessarily feeling positive. In an almost Pavlovian manner some people learn to display the attitude and behaviour expected of them.

A deeper understanding of attitude and behaviour can be gained by a study of transactional analysis (TA). I found Villere and Duet's book particularly enlightening (see Recommended Reading).

The theory of transactional analysis holds that within each of us conversations are taking place between the adult we have become, the child we were, and the parent who influenced us. During transactions with others we operate from within one of these 'ego states', and this affects the success or otherwise of the communication.

A good way of understanding TA on a very simplistic level is to imagine that everything we have ever experienced, heard, and seen is recorded in the brain. Those events that took place during the first seven to nine years of life are said to have a dramatic and lasting effect on us. In later life the recording of these events is played back from time to time. A current-day event will spark off a reaction which in turn plays the tape. Without knowing the reason why, we react to situations in varying ways, either positively or negatively. Using TA techniques it is possible to gain a clearer understanding of why we feel the way we do in certain situations; what makes us say some of the things we do (and sometimes regret); and what forces us to act in ways that at times border on being destructive.

In the process of daily communication these messages from our past can sometimes get in the way of what we are trying to achieve. No more so than with those in direct personal selling. Dependent upon each individual's own personal tape of recorded encounters, each can react differently when presented by the same customer. Trainers and man-agers also have personal perceptions which when combined with the stressful sales situation can mean a totally different view of the sales encounter to that experienced by the salesperson.

Where each, in terms of current feelings, has to do with our past, future feelings and relationships can be controlled with help, practice and understanding.

An understanding of TA can be rewarding on a personal level and also for managers. It helps to re-assess your communicative style and to cope with the findings. Children clearly cannot be held to be in the wrong until they are able to *know* they are in the wrong. Similarly, I believe that salespeople cannot be held responsible for sales failure until someone, a sales trainer, or preferably a sales manager, helps that sales-person to identify the behaviours that lead to sales failure, and then coaches new and positive behaviours. Whether the salesperson takes all this on board or not is for the salesperson alone to decide. You can coach a salesperson in successful sales behaviours but you cannot make them successful.

It is exactly this point that you have to coach managers in. They can force salespeople to increase their activity, but they cannot force them to produce bottom line results. Salespeople can be coached to carry out certain activities, and to carry out more of them, more quickly, but selling is a behaviour skill, involving emotional and social transactions, and salespeople themselves decide whether, and when, to employ those transactions.

I have found that attitudes can be changed and behaviour can be modified. A good sales trainer can help people to change their behav-iour but trainees need to keep an open mind. Those with fixed attitudes and a rigid way of looking at the world are nearly impossible to train. The older a person gets the less they will want to change and the more closed their minds will be to new ideas. Obviously, this is a generaliz-ation, but you do make your task more arduous by attempting to train closed minds.

Attitudinal training has to do with self-awareness. The more opportunities you create for salespeople to understand and to examine closely their style of communication for themselves, the greater the chances that they will embrace new ideas. Self-awareness, however, is neither for the faint-hearted trainee or indeed trainer. An integral part of self-awareness is the opportunity for self-disclosure—something salespeople are reluctant to enter into. Selling is intrinsically a macho business and signs of weakness are discouraged. This is especially so of sales managers, and trainers will find it a nerve-racking task getting together a group of sales managers to share with each other their weaknesses.

The rewards, however, can be dramatic, although perhaps not evident until some time after the training event.

Job tasks and attitudes

It is sometimes worth examining the attitude needed to carry out a particular job task. The format in Figure 4.11 shows what is required in emotional terms to carry out what seems at one level to be a simple task. For example, prospecting can be described in some detail, but, psychologically, it requires the salesperson to have a positive attitude and sufficient resilience to cope with rejection. Also, while selling is about communication and interpersonal relationships, the job of prospecting involves some fairly sterile administration as well. Lastly, most salespeople have a fear of asking for referred leads, yet this source is more often than not guaranteed to bring in business.

Job tasks	*Attitude*
Prospecting	• A positive approach to prospecting
• Using business directories	• Able to accept rejection
• Composing letters	• Accepts admin as part of the job
• Obtaining referred leads	• Not afraid of asking for referred leads

Figure 4.11   Analysis of attitude requirements

Overcoming objections and closing

Most books on selling include long passages on overcoming objections and closing techniques. In one book alone, I found seventeen different closes explained in detail. Alessandra and Wexler commented that it was small wonder that salespeople feel bad about themselves and their professional status. They were usually involved in a situation where they exploited and manipulated their prospects, using the sales techniques they had been taught.

The practice of closing techniques and of overcoming objections is dubious, to say the least. I recommend that, as a professional sales trainer, you advocate to your professional salespeople that these terms are dropped. 'Overcoming objections' sounds like a wrestling match, and 'closing' somehow smacks of dishonesty. It implies an encircling movement as though the salesperson were laying siege to a client. It also involves a considerable entourage of techniques ranging from the fantastic to the downright silly. Closing, while on one level understood by those in selling as the act of bringing a sale to a successful end, has assumed a life of its own and, in the process, fostered the belief that in the act of stringing a few words together at the appropriate moment all riches will be obtained. Closing is also a one-way benefit mechanism for salespeople. Instead, teach your salespeople to handle their prospects in the way they would like to be treated themselves. It is certain that they do not want to be 'closed' and if they did have an objection they would not like it to be 'overcome'. I don't believe that customers have objections. What they do have is insufficient knowledge to make an informed buying decision. People fail to buy, not because their objections were not overcome, but because they were not in the market to buy in the first place, or, if they were, the salesperson explained the product or service in such a way that the prospect was deterred.

There is no place in modern professional selling for overcoming objections and closing techniques. Modern professional selling is about communication at the highest level. Your training needs analysis must always include the need to train salespeople in better communication, to understand how they behave and what effect they have on other people by the way they communicate.

Communication is a matter of body language, tone of voice and words, in that order. Most of us are very poor communicators, and the inclusion of this subject as a standard training need, whether your trainees are in selling, management or digging holes in the road, should be first on any list of training needs.

Body language, or non-verbal communication, represents 65 to 75 per cent of communication, with actual words making up no more than 10 per cent. So it is necessary to spend a considerable amount of time training salespeople, whose primary function is to communicate, in how to use body language. It rarely enjoys more than a cursory mention on sales courses, because not enough sales trainers know very much about it. Learning about body language is just as difficult as learning any new language and sales trainers are as bad as salespeople when it comes to grasping the learning cudgel. But salespeople who understand body language have an enormous advantage over those who do not, although they are in a tiny minority. For the rest of us, communication is a enigmatic affair and one laden with difficulty.

Identifying body language as a training need could immediately bring you into conflict with many people, including managers who do not believe in it. You will encounter people who will say 'Body language? It's a load of rubbish! I looked at the thing once and it didn't work. It's a complete waste of time and money'. Your job as a Level One trainer is to identify the obvious that is not obvious to others.

Structured sales presentations

Is there a need for a sales structure? Many trainers advocate that having a systematic structure to a sales presentation works and in some cases is a prerequisite to sales success. Robertson produced a model which I have adapted to show three possible models, and there are many more (Figure 4.12).

The AIDA model was first introduced by Tosdal, but Johnson reasoned that this model was derived from an even earlier system advocated by Arthur Frederick Sheldon in 1901 called AIDR which stood for Attention, Interest, Desire and Resolve.

I have found that salespeople who used a structure were no more or less successful than those who did not, so there seems no point in including structured selling in your training needs analysis.

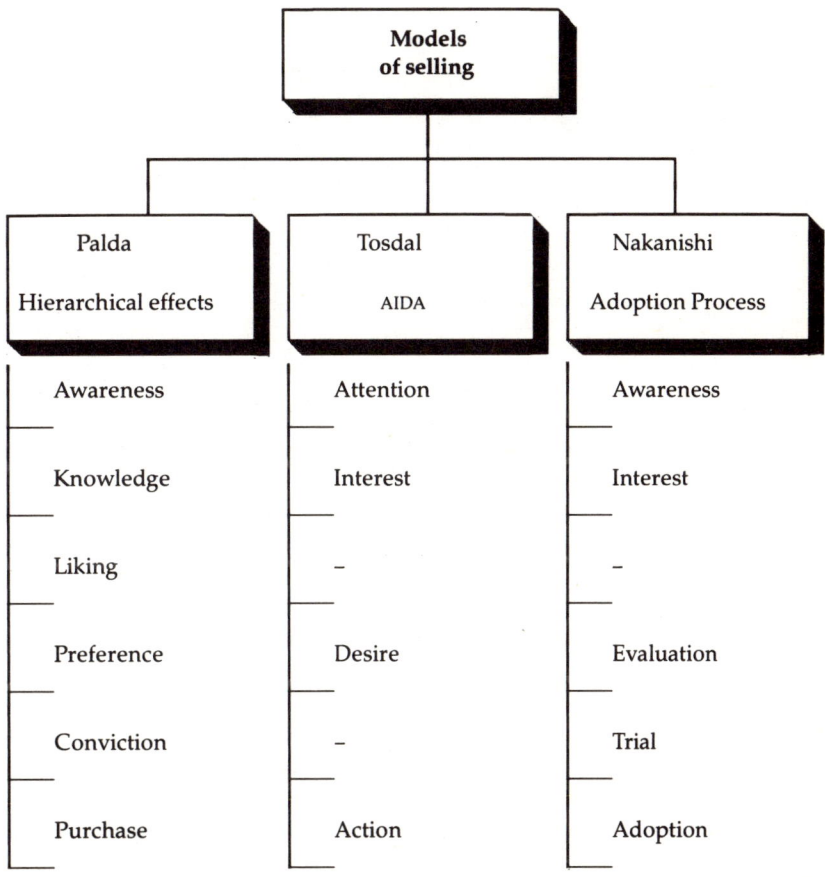

Figure 4.12 *Structured models of selling*

Key points

1 As trainers, you must be involved in the recruitment and selection process. Managers and personnel staff have an inflated expectation of what sales trainers can achieve, it seems. It is important to define exactly what the sales role is and what is expected of a salesperson before putting together a profile of what sort of person will be

recruited. The variety of sales roles is considerable and, probably, unique to each company.

2 The market *for* salespeople is far greater than the pool of professional salespeople available, so the best way is to 'grow your own'. This is expensive, but companies should examine closely the true cost of the alternatives.

3 Sales training involves focusing on knowledge, skills and attitudes. There is no evidence that increased knowledge leads to increased sales so a thorough investigation into the practice of feeding knowledge is recommended. Trainees should be encouraged to find out more for themselves. While most training courses cover product knowledge, it is suggested that the trainer also includes a section on the theory of selling in detail, as well as company politics. What goes on inside the company is in many ways just as important as the relationships that the salesperson has with potential clients.

4 The skills of selling are misunderstood by many personnel practitioners, and this is one of the main reasons for sales trainers being involved in the recruitment process. Recruiters have a tendency to produce a list of skills requirements for salespeople without fully understanding what those skills mean. Lack of the most important skill—prospecting—results in more failure than any other part of the sales job.

5 More important than knowledge or skills is attitude. A salesperson's attitude will determine whether knowledge and skills are used and is the ultimate arbiter of sales success. The most important part of attitude is keeping an open mind—by remaining flexible trainees can begin the process of any needed attitude change. By teaching salespeople to modify their behaviour it is possible to bring about a gradual change in attitude.

6 There should be no place in modern professional selling for training in the overcoming of objections or closing technique.

7 Body language training should be an integral part of any sales training programme. It represents a large part of communication but is usually ignored by trainers and managers alike.

Recommended reading

Braysich, J. *Body Language*, Joseph Braysich & Assoc. 1979.

Greenberg, H. and J. 'Predicting sales success—myths and reality', *Personnel Journal* Dec. 1975.

Hillibrand, M. *Source Credibility and the Persuasive Process*, Harvard University 1964.

Mayer J. and H. Greenberg, 'What makes a good salesman?' *Harvard Business Review* July 1964.

References

Chrissy, W. *Salesmanship: the personal force in marketing*, Wiley 1982.

Drucker, P. *People and Performance*, Heinemann 1977.

Festinger, L. 'Behavioural support for opinion change', *Public Opinion Quarterly*. Vol. 28. 1964.

Guion, R.M. *Personnel Testing*, McGraw-Hill 1965.

Herzberg, F. *The Motivation to Work*, John Wiley & Sons 1959.

Johnson, E.M., D.L. Hurtz and E. Sheuning, *Sales management: concepts, practices, and cases*, McGraw-Hill 1986.

McGregor, D. *The Human Side of Enterprise*, McGraw-Hill 1960.

Maslow, A. 'A theory of human motivation', *Psychological Review* 1943.

Nykodyn *et al.* 'Selection systems for sales', *Journal of Management* Aug. 1986.

Rae, L. *The Skills of Human Relations Training*, Gower 1985.

Robertson, T. *Innovative Behaviour and Communication*, Holt, Reinhart 1971.

Sheldon, A.F. *see* A.R. Hahn, 'Selling's path-finder', *Sales Management* December 1952.

Shostack, G.L. 'Handling the cult of the professional', *American Banker* April 1982.

Tosdal, H.R. *Principles of Personal Selling*, McGraw-Hill 1925.

Villere M.F. and C.P. Duet, *Successful Selling through TA*, Prentice Hall 1980.

5 The sales trainer

This chapter deals with the following questions:

- Who should deliver the sales training?
- What skills, knowledge and experience should the sales trainer have?
- What role if any do external training consultants have?

The central sales trainer

The main influences on the effectiveness of the sales training event are the trainer, the methods used, and the type of evaluation and follow-up. Of these, the single most important ingredient in any sales training programme is not the material, the venue, or the products being sold—it is unquestionably the sales trainer.

A good sales trainer will work with the most sales-resistant people, succeed in the most appalling conditions, and teach people how to sell the worst product range imaginable. I do not say that the results of that training will be sustainable long-term. I doubt whether the training will work even the next day, but while it lasts a good sales trainer will make people believe in themselves, the company, and the product. I fully recognize the limitations of sales trainers. The problem is that managers, and especially those who are not sales managers, do not understand those limitations.

Sales training in isolation does not work. All sales training provided by a central sales trainer is merely a foundation. If effective it can be a solid foundation. As parents we firmly believe in a good start in life for our children, and in giving them solid foundations upon which to build their lives. The provision of central sales training is the same for trainees. It can, depending on the sales trainer, provide trainees with the groundwork upon which they can build a successful professional sales career. The important requirement is that the sales trainer has to be of the highest quality, and this is where your troubles begin.

Most companies look upon the sales training function as a support service, one which they will seek to fill as cheaply as possible. In sales training you definitely get what you pay for. It has been said by Veevers, Hope and Knights, and others that many in-house training programmes fall far short of the mark because trainers are used who were not previously top salespeople.

Training departments seem prone to receive people who have failed at something else; the solution is to put them in the training department. But one thing is certain: a sales training department is the last place you should put a failed salesperson. Would you be happy to take investment advice from someone who paupered themselves following their own investment strategy? Putting a failed salesperson in charge of new sales trainees will guarantee that they too will learn how to fail.

No one, neither the manager nor the sales trainer, should be allowed anywhere near front-line salespeople, if they themselves have not been successful at selling. As Buzzotto and Lefton pointed out in 1980, the sales trainer has to be able to sell the idea of learning and behavioural change to trainees. A good sales trainer creates an environment conducive to learning. A good sales trainer is also able to adapt training to the needs of a particular trainee group on the spur of the moment. That is why I do not like rigid training packages or selling structures of the type you see advertised, promising instant success for a minimal outlay. Selling and sales training is a continuous process that takes a lifetime to learn and become good at. It takes energy and perseverance and most people fail at it because they neither understand it nor are able to put up with the difficulties encountered.

When you construct a sales training programme, the primary objective is to get the best front-line sales trainer that money can buy. You must be wary of picking up a good sales trainer too cheaply. A good sales trainer costs a lot of money. This is probably a good moment to put this book down and take a look at the sales training staff you have in your company. Examine closely how much they are paid in relation to (a) other training functions, and (b) most other head office jobs. Then take out an organizational chart of your company and see where sales trainers stack up against other head office managers. If the structure does not closely reflect that in Figure 5.1 then you still have a long way to go. The sales trainer should have the ear and commitment of the managing director of the company. Sales training is an emotional process and as such has a tenuous relationship with many other company central functions. Those not up to the constant pressure of an organization steeped in a sales culture will constantly try to demote or decry sales training as being either not important or too costly. Without the visible support of the managing director and a display of the importance of the function, it is doomed to fail.

Once you have the right sales trainer, everything else will fall into place. What you must avoid is employing any person in a sales training or sales management role who knows the theory but has not had the practice. If your business is retailing, then the trainer must have worked behind a sales counter. If your business is direct personal selling, then the trainer must have knocked on doors. The sales trainer must have credibility, and in selling the only credibility they can have is to have sold successfully.

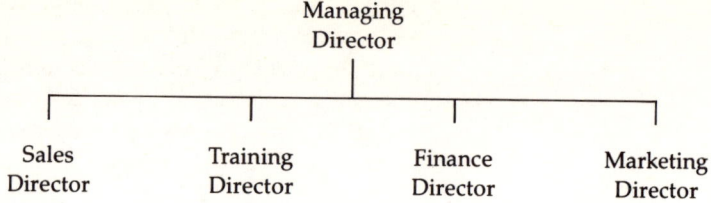

Figure 5.1 *Company structure*

I cannot guarantee that employing the best salesperson as the sales trainer will always work, no more than making the best salesperson into a sales manager always works, but it does seem a reasonable place to start. Training skills are important, but these can be taught. The techniques can be learned.

The best place to find the ideal sales trainer is in the top ten to fifteen per cent of your sales team. This means that you will have to compensate them for what they would lose in sales commission. Your investment will be returned a thousand-fold. The problem is that sales training in many companies is not sufficiently rewarded to attract the best salespeople and poor salespeople are often put into sales training roles simply to get them out of the field. If they are not earning very much then a sales training job can look very attractive. For the best salespeople, the only way to get out of selling is to move into sales management, where at least the rewards are greater than in sales training. Good salespeople are no different from poor salespeople—they also want to get out of front-line selling every now and then. The tragedy of it is that many good salespeople end up failing in sales management and return to selling having lost their confidence, when a career in sales training would have allowed them to build upon their success.

Good salespeople need little training to be good sales trainers. With continual study and practice they can become great sales trainers.

If you want the best sales team
get the best sales trainer

Rules for sales trainers

The sales trainer acts as a role model for all new trainees. New recruits are influenced by the attitude and image of the trainer and, especially in the early days, learn very quickly what the internal rules of the company are by the way the sales trainers conduct themselves. There are therefore some occasionally unpalatable areas of the trainer's image that should be addressed.

The way you look is important. The way you act is vital. In sales training, for many people, you are attempting to change their behaviour. The first thing they will do is look at you, and from that point your training event could become a disaster. If you look sloppy, are overweight, and cannot put a convincing argument together, then why should they listen to you? Selling requires more than just turning up for work. It is the most undervalued of professions, primarily because those in it do not realize that it takes more to be a professional salesperson than just talking. Selling, especially in the last decade of the twentieth century and into the next, will involve the ability to communicate at the highest level. It requires those in the profession to be constantly aware of the influence that their verbal and non-verbal behaviour has on prospects. Sales trainers are no different from salespeople in that they too have something to sell.

In a sales situation, and particularly in the first few minutes of a sales presentation, prospects are exposed to a stimulation of the five human senses of taste, touch, sight, sound and smell. In particular, the senses of sight and sound are of great importance. The important of looks in selling cannot be overemphasized. I don't mean glamorous good looks but the initial impression that we give others in relation to our dress, our overall look, the way we are groomed and how we act. Philippa Davies says that the order in which we notice and react to other people's characteristics is:

- skin colour
- gender
- size
- facial expression
- eye contact
- hair
- build
- clothes
- movement

To this list I would add smoking. Good sales trainers do not smoke. Smoking shows a total lack of judgement on the part of the trainer. Sales training, as we shall see, involves a great deal of emphasis on attitude, motivation, feeling well about yourself, and image. Smoking shows dependency on something outside an individual's control and will send confusing messages to trainees. Part of the job of a sales trainer is to be larger than life. The sales trainer is a role model for trainees and has an enormous influence on the way life is seen and practised. If you do not like this sort of responsibility then do not be a sales trainer. Sales training is a high-profile job. You are on show every minute of every day and have a tremendous amount of responsibility and accountability for the way in which the training programme is viewed, accepted and acted upon.

The second sense, of sound, is just as important for salespeople and especially so for sales trainers. A sales trainer might have the best material in the world, may look the part, and have all the experience and knowledge needed, but if they sound boring, they will be boring. You know how draining it is to sit and listen to boring speakers, even when the content is interesting, and yet many sales trainers seem oblivious of the need to develop a clear and interesting speaking voice that uses all the range of possibilities in voice tone and pitch. For this reason it is important that trainers are regularly assessed by their peers and practise what they preach by recording and listening to their training events as often as possible.

Consultants

Some companies use external sales training consultants either to design the programme or to deliver the training. Other companies will use external sales training companies by sending their staff to them periodically for training. There are advantages and disadvantages in using external sales training consultants.

Disadvantages

One major problem that the use of external sales training consultants presents is that it can send mixed messages to the staff. The company expects the highest levels of performance from its salespeople and yet displays that at a training and management level it is unable to cope without external help. If this is the case, then why does the company not employ external salespeople to sell its products and services?

It has often been said that consultants are most useful in times of change, because staff more readily accept change which appears to be initiated by external sources. There is some mileage in this but it is also indicative of suspect management, especially in matters to do with sales training. Many managers seem incapable of recognizing that their sales teams are crammed full of talent, knowledge and experience which, if harnessed properly, could provide the company with the help it needs. A properly run sales culture endorses and welcomes change as a constituent part and subscribes to the belief that all individuals need to grow and develop.

If your staff are prone to resisting change, and most are, then your organizational climate could benefit enormously from a good sales trainer.

A further disadvantage of using external consultants is that they learn while you pay. In many cases the consultants get more out of their involvement with your company than you do, yet you have the privilege of paying. No matter what they say to you, they will use this experience to the benefit of other firms, in the same way that they have used the experience of other firms to benefit you. Many will have standard packages that they will cleverly alter to suit your company. Why not promote to a senior position in your company a good salesperson to head up the sales training department? Why companies are willing to pay huge sums of money to people outside the company to learn about the business, when there are numerous people already working for the company that just need some encouragement and development escapes me.

Advantages

External sales training consultants who are interested in making the company self-sufficient will bring with them a breadth of experience from other companies that could be invaluable. I stress that they should be concerned about making the company's sales trainers self-sufficient and I would warn against employing any consultant who does not make this a prerequisite for becoming involved. Any reputable sales training consultants should want to prove they can help the company grow its own sales trainers in the long run. Those that do not have this as a clause in their proposals will not be on the same wavelength as you, and you will probably teach them more about sales training than they will teach you. Use only consultants who are interested in tackling the organizational problems attached to sales training and not those who provide you with sales training technique and off-the-shelf packages. These can be bought anywhere, and eventually can be done in-house, anyway.

Consultants, in theory, will deter your company from making the same mistakes as other companies they have dealt with. This, of course, depends on which consultant you employ and what experience they have. Remember, there are many companies that do not know the first thing about sales training and, therefore, there are bound to be a number of consultants who make a good living providing these companies with what they want, without taking account of what they need.

Good consultants should be able to improve and develop the knowledge and skills of your sales trainer, and this is their main strength. Use the consultant to train the trainer, and in this way training is cascaded downward. Using an external sales training consultant to train your staff or managers will impress both, but it could also make it impossible for staff sales trainers to assert themselves later.

Senior managers within the company will love external consultants. They cost a lot and, because of their experience, will be able to say all the right things at the right time and consequently stroke the egos of their paymasters. Similarly, staff being trained by a good external consultant will feel good about the amount of money being invested in them. If the internal sales trainer held a senior management appointment in the first place then I am certain that these same perceptions about the importance and quality of training would also prevail.

The best course to follow is for the sales trainer to be trained by the consultant outside the company. The trainer can watch the consultant in action elsewhere. The consultant can help the trainer to develop a programme and in effect become a private tutor 'marking' the trainer's work and refining it when appropriate.

effect become a private tutor 'marking' the trainer's work and refining it when appropriate.

A vital function of consultants is that they help to improve the image of the internal trainer and they must support the trainer's advancement within the company at all costs. In effect, the consultant's job is to sell the trainer to the company. Eventually, as the trainer takes on more responsibility for design, the consultant is used as a sounding board for ideas and problems.

The sales manager

Having decided on the sales trainer, it should be recognized that the sales trainer and the training provided centrally is only one part of a successful training programme. Effective sales training programmes contain a number of elements (see Figure 5.2). We have already examined the type of person responsible for pulling the whole thing together and I will expand on this central role later. For now let us look at the role of the sales manager, who is a vitally important person in the field training element.

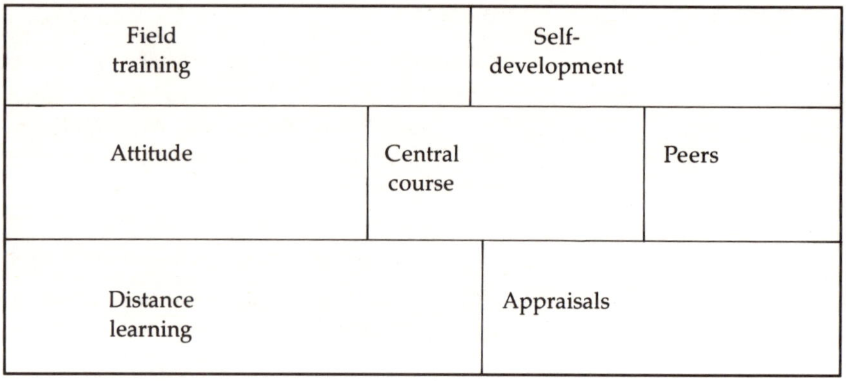

Field training		Self-development	
Attitude	Central course		Peers
Distance learning		Appraisals	

Figure 5.2   *Elements of sales training*

Without doubt, the single most important and influential part of any sales training programme is the involvement of the sales manager. No matter what happens on a sales training course, or what level of training the central sales training provides, the ultimate success of the programme rests with the line manager. The line manager can undo in two minutes what a sales trainer has spent weeks putting together. The line manager can also be the final catalyst for reinforcing everything covered centrally, and can ensure that the transition from theory to practice goes ahead without any hitches.

I have been fortunate enough to meet a large number of senior managers of large successful sales forces, some numbering thousands, in Britain, the United States and Europe. In all cases, I took the opportunity to ask them what was the single most important component of sales success, and without exception they said 'the sales manager'. I have also been unfortunate enough to meet a great many senior managers of unsuccessful sales teams and when I asked what was the greatest problem with the sales team, in many cases they said 'sales training'. There is a popular misconception that sales training can put everything right. It is only part of the system, the most important part of which is the sales manager.

A sign of a poor sales manager is one who believes that all matters relating to training are for trainers. Level One trainers provide foundation sales training for salespeople and then train sales managers to continue that training in the field. Lidstone, in particular, continually refers to the need for sales managers to be able to train and says that if managers cannot train, they cannot manage. I would agree, and place the blame for the high labour turnover rates in salesforces in Britain squarely at the door of an army of untrained unprofessional sales managers.

This area of sales management involvement is crucial to the success of any sales training programme. If you are starting with a clean sheet, in a company where no sales training of any merit has been carried out in the past, your first and only task is to train managers to be sales trainers, and until you have achieved that goal, keep away from the existing salesforce. The prime function of a sales manager is to train the company's own salespeople to achieve those organizational goals that the manager cannot achieve alone. Sales managers are the most important sales trainers in any company. They must be able to sell, be able to train, and be able to motivate. As Giles says, managers should conduct training events, and deal directly with the problems concerning motivation of salespeople.

For this to work, it is important that the sales manager has been a successful salesperson. If sales managers cannot sell, have not sold, and cannot therefore teach their people to sell, you have an impossible task in front of you. I have heard all the arguments about sales managers not needing a successful record, and it just does not stack up. The person who is in the front line deserves to be managed by someone who knows what they are talking about, can relate to the job and the salesperson, and can motivate that salesperson to want to sell.

The most important function of the sales manager is to train salespeople how to do the job. Most of this will take place when sales managers are out on calls with salespeople, carrying out what is known as field visits. Every sales meeting should also contain an element of sales training. The first thing on the agenda for any meeting of any kind between sales manager and salespeople must be sales training.

I know salespeople do not want sales training, but that must not deter the company from constantly providing it. Children do not want to go to school, but we grown-ups know it is good for them. Sometimes you, as a sales training manager, have to treat salespeople and their managers like children. They do not know it today, but forcing them to have sales training on a regular basis will help them to grow up strong, healthy and profitable.

It is essential that the messages given out on any central sales course are immediately repeated in the field by a sales manager. Central sales training, by the nature of the event, is theoretical. The only way that you can be sure that it works is to repeat the event in the field and the only person capable of doing this is the sales manager. This transference of learning to the field is central to the successful sales training programme. Would you teach someone to drive in a classroom and then allow them to drive on their own on the road? Selling is also a skill that can be learned both in theoretical terms and in practice. The effect of not ensuring that sales training is transferred to the field can be as catastrophic to the sales health of the company as an unpractised driver can be to pedestrians and other drivers.

Obviously, this all involves time and managers are keen to stress that time is money. They will offer the most coherent argument about lack of time to train people, how much paperwork they have to do, how many sales meetings and business lunches they have to attend. I guarantee that if they did no paperwork for a month, and attended no meetings or business lunches for a year, it would have no detrimental effect on company results, but it could help company profitability. If they traded all these activities for sales training events with their salespeople, both in the field and in the classroom, but with an emphasis on the former, it would have a dramatic positive effect on results. Try it. Do it. Insist on it.

The resistance you meet will be enormous. Sales managers are notorious for finding reasons not to train their salespeople. I will explain in the next chapter how to set up a field visit system that will help you to confirm that training is being continually carried out. In Stafford and Grant's book, *Effective Sales Management*, they say that the average sales manager spends less that 50 per cent of work time in the field training the sales team. Further, the authors believe that many field 'days' are in fact half-days, that there are always problems in the office that managers have unexpectedly to return to. My own research shows that most sales managers spend less than 20 per cent of their time in the field with their salespeople. This is recorded time. When I delved more deeply I found that what sales managers call a day's field visit probably lasts no more than one or two hours.

Sales training as a resource should be switched entirely from sales training of salespeople to sales training of sales managers. To do this you have to sell the benefits of a controlled system to the managing director. This is not as daunting as it sounds. The MD should agree that most of a manager's time should be spent with the sales team. You could also start a research project to investigate the effectiveness of field visits and managerial involvement in sales training. To do this you need data, and to collect data you need returns from managers. To persuade them to provide the information you could introduce a system such as that shown in Chapter Seven.

Key points

1 While the methods used, and the follow-up, are extremely important parts of any successful sales training programme, the central sales trainer is without doubt the main influence on the training event.
2 To establish credibility and get the most out of the training event, the sales trainer must also have been a successful salesperson.
3 The sales trainer acts as a role model for trainees. The image the trainer portrays is taken as the 'norm' for the company.
4 External consultants should only be used to train and advise trainers.
5 Central sales training is merely a foundation. The sales manager is the integral ingredient in any successful sales training programme.

Recommended reading

Bennett, R. *Improving Trainer Effectiveness*, Gower 1988.
Craig R. L. and L. Kelly. *Sales training handbook: A guide to developing sales performance*, Prentice Hall 1990.

References

Buzzotta V. R. and R. E. Lefton, *Effective Selling through Psychology*, Wiley Interscience 1977.
Davies, P. *Your Total Image: how to communicate success*, Piatkus 1990.
Giles, G. B. *Marketing*, M & E Handbooks 1978.
Hope V., D. Knights and H. Wilmott. 'The ambivalence of personnel in life assurance: the challenge of change', *Personnel Review*. 17, 1. 1988.
Lidstone, J. *Training Salesmen on the Job*, Gower Press 1975.
Stafford J. and C. Grant. *Effective Sales Management*, Heinemann 1986.
Veevers, P. 'Time to look back', *Training Officer* July 1983.

6 The central training programme

This chapter aims to answer the following questions:

- What part does the central training programme play in the overall provision of sales training?
- What elements are contained in the programme?
- Is there a structured approach to selling that can be used in the central training programme?

Role

The provision of central training has two main functions:

1 Training the sales manager, and
2 Providing foundation sales training for salespeople.

Learning is a slow process, and the acquisition of new skills requires a great deal of effort and time. It is a measure of a professional career that it takes years of study, application and practice before it can be said that professional status is reached. And yet organizations give their salespeople no more than between one to five days central sales training before they start the job, and then expect them to perform immediately. Those who complain that selling is not treated as a profession are their own worst enemies.

The provision of a central training event, whether of one day or twelve months duration, should be seen only as a foundation upon which to build a professional sales career. Central events are merely the stimulus for salespeople to develop themselves, and for sales managers to use as a touchpaper for further training. Central training on its own cannot and does not work. It is far better not to have any training at all, than to have central training in isolation.

Selling skills are difficult to acquire and easy to lose when not used regularly. Selling is also an emotional skill, that requires salespeople to expose their feelings at every contact with a prospect. In personal selling, in particular, there tends to be more rejection than acceptance, and it is quite normal for salespeople to seek practices and opportunities to avoid prospect contact and put off potential rejection. Unless selling skills are practised regularly they tend to deteriorate as salespeople and sales managers involve themselves in administrative functions as a place to hide.

For example, think of how much time salespeople and managers put into finding new sources of business, refining advertisements of their services, and trying to put the onus for prospecting on someone else's shoulders. Why? Because they do not like contacting people and selling to them. *Most salespeople and most sales managers do not enjoy customer contact, unless the customer has instigated the sales process.*

Exposing feelings is a dangerous business, and all of us avoid it like the plague. That is why it is vitally important to make sales training a continuous process and to have managers deliver sales training at every available opportunity.

People acquire skills through repetition, as Figure 6.1 shows. The more often a skill is practised the nearer to the top of the scale a person gets. At the bottom end people have no skill and are unaware of the lack of a skill. Through repetition and practice the training programme's aim is to make people aware of their shortcomings and build a desire to improve their level of skills until such time as they are proficient, but still have to concentrate most of the time. At the top end of the scale people have acquired a skill through repetition to the extent that they are able to use that skill without concentration as though it were a natural talent. There are those who do have natural talent, but they are so few and far between as not to register in a sample of the population. Those born with natural sales talent will most probably not join your company, anyway. They have no need of your company.

Why are we re-training? (handwritten margin note)

Training sales managers

Sales managers will form the main thrust of your sales training initiatives. As mentioned earlier, the purpose of any central training event or programme is to provide a foundation upon which trainees can base their learning. Most learning will take place on the job, and the greatest influence on the quality and quantity of learning achieved will rest totally with the sales manager. This requires the central training function to teach the sales manager how to be an effective trainer. Some people call it coaching, and there are analogies between sales trainers and sporting coaches.

As with a coach, the sales trainer attempts to get the best possible performance from a trainee at a critical moment. With athletes, the job of the coach is not to bring that performance to a peak too early or too late, and the same applies to the sales coach. The sales manager's job is to coach salespeople so that they peak during the sales presentation. This is the moment of highest skill application. All other functions of a salesperson can be done by machines or other people and can be classified as administrative functions. The sales presentation, however, is for the salesperson the FA Cup final, the Wimbledon championship or the Grand National. Success at this point is the culmination of knowledge acquisition and skills practice, and reinforces attitude development.

Definition of client meeting (handwritten margin note)

The function of sales managers, in all their dealings with the salesperson, is to ensure that all efforts are focused on that moment when the salesperson

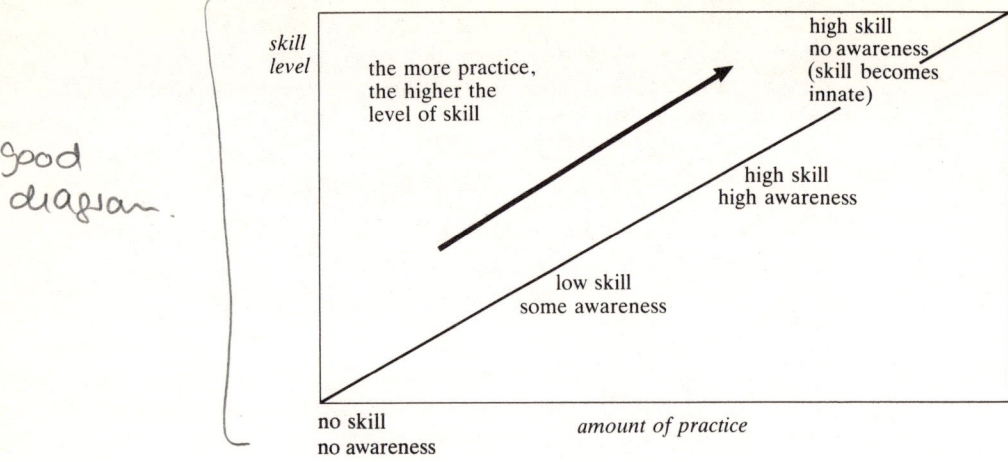

good diagram.

Figure 6.1   *How to acquire a skill*

and customer are communicating, either on the telephone or face to face. All other forms of contact can be done by non-salespeople.

Before you run a central training event for salespeople you should put the sales manager through at least a condensed version of the training course. If there is time available, and I suggest strongly that time should be made, the ideal would be to put the sales manager through the whole programme step by step. Whatever you do, this link between central sales training and the continuation of that training in the field is essential to the success and ultimate effectiveness of the entire sales training programme.

Two major reasons for this are that skills can only be learned through repetition and practice, and that, in the eyes of trainees, there has to be consistency between what is taught centrally and what is taught in the field.

Repetition and practice

There is direct correlation between practice and level of skill achievement (see Figure 6.1). The job of a sales trainer is to move people from the bottom left-hand side of the model to the top right-hand side of the model. This critical period is often the time when sales training fails, as trainees either progress too slowly for their self-esteem and the approval of their managers or, in many cases, deteriorate in performance (see Figure 6.2). Ask any sportsman, however, what happens when they are learning a new technique and you will find the same process. A tennis player trying to add a new technique, such as changing a backhand shot, will often see an initial reduction in performance. Or a concert violinist learning a new piece will, to untrained ears, sound like a novice for quite some time before eventually turning in a virtuoso performance. The trick is to expose this reduction in performance on the practice pitch (classroom) and not on the playing field (on a live call).

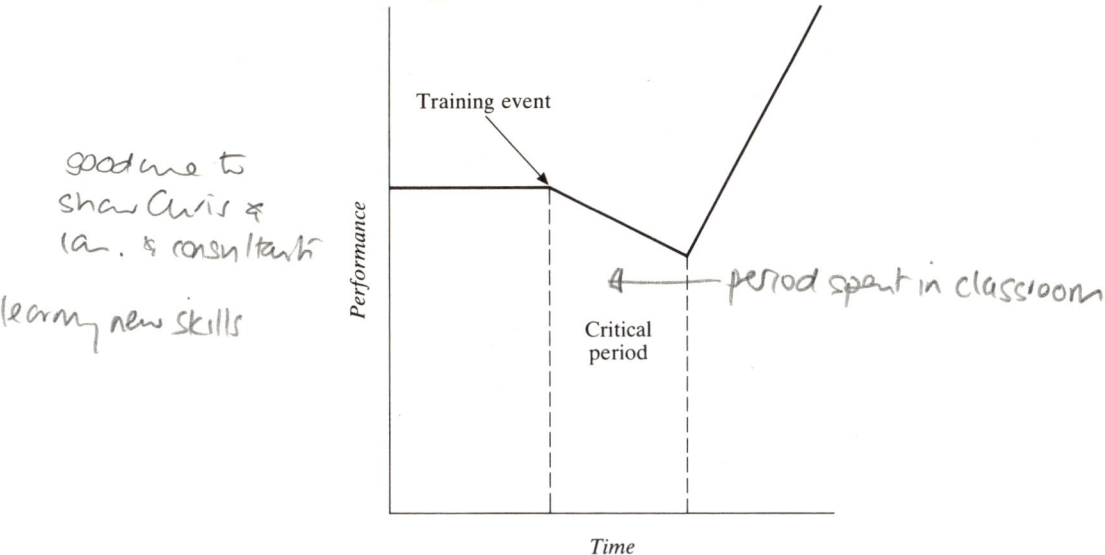

good me to
shaw Chris &
Ian. & consultant

→ learning new skills

Figure 6.2 Performance movements during acquisition of new skill

It is usual, however, for salespeople and managers to give up long before this process is complete and so you need to explain in detail how the process works and why it is important for them, the sales managers, to assist you in the total sales training programme. On a central sales training event you may only be able to move trainees a small way up the model. Unless the sales manager picks this up immediately after the training event, the risk is that you will have completely wasted the company's training resources as trainees slip back to old and comfortable ways. Like the footballer on the pitch of play, it is no fun to be barracked by supporters, colleagues and opposition players as you learn your new skill and appear to miss golden opportunities.

It is far easier to turn in an average performance than to go for excellence.

The sales manager has to encourage practice and help trainees cope with the frustration of skills learning through the difficult initial stages. Eventually a high performance will be achieved through the conscious practice of new skills. Through continual reinforcement and learning, salespeople can display all the behavioural hallmarks of successful selling which to others appear to be innate skills. Only the salesperson and the manager know that these 'natural' traits are the result of a conscious application of skills learned over a long period of time. There will be those who move eventually to the top of the model and are able to display those high-level skills without thinking about it. In some rare cases there will be salespeople who are already like that, but it is unlikely that they will be working for you. Your only hope is that you can coach people to within a ten to twenty per cent shortfall of maximum performance.

The ideal opportunity for sales managers to help their charges acquire this high level of skills achievement is through field training, which is covered in the next chapter.

Organizing the central training event

If the training event is to cover product knowledge then the following format should be used:

1 Provide trainees with self-study material before the event.
2 Test their knowledge at some stage in the field, either by means of a computer-based testing system if available, or a test administered by line managers.
3 Run the training event, or the part containing product knoweldge.
4 Test knowledge at the end of the event or course.
5 Set trainees post-course self-study material.
6 Having involved managers in course preparation and trained them to train, make sure they set training and assessment tasks for their trainees. Provide them with the necessary testing material.

Using this methodology you will be able to determine how much people know before the training event; how much they learned during the training event; how much they retained after the training event; and what further study requirements there are.

Self-study

A cornerstone of your training programme should be a self-study pack containing the following elements:

- A complete description of all the company's products and services;
- The company's mission statement; the training policy statement; a detailed description of the year's business plans and where salespeople's and sales managers' responsibilities and accountabilities lie;
- Case studies of sales situations and sales scripts, including a bibliography for further reading;
- Self-tests.

Without doubt, the best learning takes place when it has been self-initiated. The problem I have found in all sales teams, however, is lack of motivation to do any self-study. Salespeople and sales managers are notorious for wanting spoon-fed training. It is rare to find people who are concerned with improving their minds and their skills through constant study and practice. Although your task may be extremely difficult, it is not impossible. Fostering an environment in which people accept responsibility for self-development is not easy and the majority of trainers I have met usually give up. Level One trainers see it through.

A large part of creating the right environment in which people want to learn and practise their skills has to do with motivation and I have devoted a separate chapter to the subject of motivation and its important role in a sales training programme.

Venue

Every company should have an in-house residential training venue. Using hotels is distracting for trainees and overly expensive. In large hotels, your training event can feel like being in a sausage machine of learning. Only the hotel will benefit from your investment. The average delegate rate can be quite reasonable, but when you add on all the extras it can become a waste of resources. Ask yourself this question often: 'Does my company's provision of training benefit other people's companies more than it benefits mine?'

X
disagree

Also, if your company does not have an internal training facility then it displays to the staff a lack of belief in training. It says to everyone that training is a separate event, something that you have to leave the company premises for.

Maybe your premises are tight on space—so what? Cut the dining room in half, reduce the size of the reception area, stop hoarding stationery, but get a training room. It is not unusual for companies to devote lots of space to storing paperclips but not to allocate space for training its employees. Let everyone work from home rather than not have any space for training.

When you have managed to get a training room make sure that it is light, that you can control the climate, and that the furniture is comfortable. If it means delivering two less training days per year or even one whole week less, invest in some decent furniture that shows your people you care for their comfort; it will also help to maintain attention. It is hard enough getting people on a training course to concentrate without introducing an extra obstacle to learning in the form of uncomfortable seating. Learning on training courses is a precarious affair with most learning having disappeared within forty-eight hours of the course. Do not let your course be remembered for being uncomfortable. It could be the greatest false economy.

Interruptions Do not allow any interruptions during any course for any reason. There are no such things as emergencies. If things have happened elsewhere, there is nothing the trainee can do to undo that. This business of interruptions is especially prevalent among sales managers, who use the telephone as their particular 'worry blanket'. I know some sales managers who would have a limb cut off rather than not make or receive a telephone call at least once every half-hour. There is an increasing number of managers taking and making telephone calls in their cars. It is nonsense to assume that a manager, or a salesperson, cannot be away from interruptions for at least eight hours of any day. If their jobs are so important and demanding then they should either not be on courses in the first place, or make and receive all calls between midnight and 5 a.m. Ask them to imagine that a new government decree says telephone lines are only available between these times. How important would they then rate telephone calls?

X Salespeople, as a group especially, will use the telephone during courses as a distraction or a confirmation of their importance. But ask them to make a live sales call on the telephone to secure an appointment and it is amazing how many reasons there are for not doing it.

Spare everyone the embarrassment and do not have telephones in the training room, near the training room, or preferably in the same building. Save all messages for the end of the day, and instruct those taking messages that the trainee, manager or not, will not be given the message till after 5 p.m. and to take a contact number for after that time. Emergencies are extremely rare and you will recognize one when it comes along.

Breaks

Take a break every forty-five minutes and allow one and a half hours for lunch. This lunch-time break should allow time for trainees to study what has been delivered in the morning, or to prepare something for the afternoon session. These breaks are meant to permit the trainee to absorb the information and the trainer to rest. Learning begins to be ineffective after forty-five minutes and the trainer becomes less convincing.

During these breaks make everyone stand up and leave the room if possible. Provide continuous refreshments just outside the training room so that people do not have far to go and also make sure that toilets are close.

Training is not meant to be an endurance course for anyone—trainers or trainees. As a professional trainer you are entrusted with using your judgement to determine the best learning environment for trainees and not to fill in time. Many training courses start early, run late, and spill over into evenings simply to justify the expense. The brain has a limitless capacity for storing information but without recharging the batteries we tend to lose the map telling us where that information is stored. Short bursts of training in limited amounts are far more effective than endless hours of time filling. There is no need to work evenings. Trainees are entitled to their free time and so are trainers. The learning environment will be greatly enhanced by allowing people to rest each night. There is no gain in trying to work tired minds.

The problem is the executive disease prevalent in much of corporate Britain. At times it appears that being *at* work is far more important than what you *do* at work. If you are any good at what you do then you should be able to achieve more in ten minutes than most people achieve in a week.

That is why field training is so important and can be so effective. Providing the foundation has been laid, half an hour of field coaching can be equal to five days classroom training, depending on who is doing it, and how the event is structured.

Training schedules

I recommend that you construct a training event schedule similar to that shown in Figure 6.3, but I would caution you against rigidly adhering to it. The only people I know who follow strict training agendas are those who are terrified to deviate because they do not know their subject well enough. Most poor trainers with little experience of the subject lock into training schedules and follow them to the last detail. It usually happens in large training organizations that have a standard package to sell and

Training Schedule						
Session	Time	Monday	Tuesday	Wednesday	Thursday	Friday
1	9 am to 9.45 am	personal presentation	personal presentation	personal presentation	personal presentation	personal presentation
2	10 am to 10.45 am					
3	11 am to 11.45 am					
4	12 noon 1.30 pm	lunch and study	lunch and study	lunch and study	lunch and study	lunch and study
5	1.30 pm to 2.15 pm	personal presentation	personal presentation	personal presentation	personal presentation	personal presentation
6	2.30 pm to 3.15 pm					review and test
7	3.30 pm to 4.15 pm					
8	4.30 pm to 5.15 pm					
9	5.30 pm to 6 pm	review and test	review and test	review and test	review and test	

Figure 6.3 *Schedule for training event*

use clones to deliver them. It always happens inside companies that buy external training programmes. In many cases the trainer does not understand the full programme anyway and would panic if it did not follow the set pattern. I've often heard trainers say 'We're running behind here, so if we can cover that later, let's press on'. Participation is important, and in many ways group discussion can be far more rewarding and lasting than structured training sessions. Obviously, any departure from your plan must be relevant, but you should be prepared to alter your course in tune with the needs of the group. Most of you will, in any case, plan a course for the average or ideal trainee. When you find one, let me know. As sales situations change, so will courses. Remember, your course is only a small part of a total training programme. If you employ a detailed feedback system to managers, you should be able to let them know where to pick up the training, at the point you left off.

Your training event should be dynamic and alter according to the audience. That is why you need an experienced salesperson as much as an experienced trainer. A good salesperson will know what to say and when to say it, as well as how to say it. They will deal with questions as they come up and not give the usual response: 'That's a good question, and I will deal with that later when we cover that subject'. Not having a query answered is distracting and loses the opportunity for the sales trainer to show that he knows his subject inside out, which he should do. If you are asked a question during a course—answer it immediately.

The sample schedule is meant to be a guide but I would recommend that certain elements are pre-set, namely the personal presentations by trainees in the morning, the review and test at the end of the day, and the start times. Lunch and the personal presentation after lunch will depend on what happened in the morning and you may find you need to shorten the lunch period or drop the presentation afterwards to gain extra time. Provided your training sessions are short, you can afford to shorten the lunch break.

A word about starting on time: when your agenda says nine o'clock start, then start at nine o'clock, whether anybody is there or not. Anyone not in place by your start time will have to wait till the next break. There are certain disciplines in selling which are of paramount importance to success, and being on time is one of them. Your training courses should reflect the importance of time-keeping by starting on time. Do not penalize those who are on time by holding up the start, while rewarding those who are late by waiting for them.

The personal presentation at the beginning of the day, and the test at the end, are important events in establishing the right frame of mind. If trainees know they have to make a personal presentation each morning then the chances are they will try to get a good night's sleep and be in the right frame of mind for the rest of the day. A test at the end of each day should also guarantee that most trainees stay awake and make notes.

Trainees should be made aware that their performance on the training course is all part of their probationary period, and that you will be reporting on their performance at the end of the course. This is discussed in more detail in Chapter 9.

Finish early on Fridays. Friday afternoon is a good time for the trainer to reflect on what happened and make some initial notes before the euphoria of the weekend settles in. Trainees appreciate getting home on time, and in any case by lunch time on Friday they have already left you, even though the body may still be present. As the saying goes, 'The lights are on, but there's nobody at home'.

Smoking   Do not allow smoking on your courses. Not only is smoking a sign of poor judgement on the part of those selling and those training, but it can produce an extremely uncomfortable training environment. It also helps to distract from what is being taught.

Trainer's guides Discipline yourself to produce a trainer's guide for each day (Figure 6.4). It helps you to focus with some clarity on what you are trying to achieve, and will keep you organized. It also helps someone else if for some reason you are not there.

The training guide should show in detail the methodologies to be used and you should seek to present a varied approach each day. People learn through having all their senses stimulated, and you should try to lock into all of them across a full day's programme in order to vary the pace and keep attention focused on the objective of the programme.

Methods of training include:

- Role plays
- Discussions
- Video playback
- Syndicate work
- Case studies
- Films
- Quizzes
- Personal presentations
- Formal tests
- Trainer's lectures

The more variety you can offer each day the better. Do not be afraid of repeating the same message over and over using a different medium. It will help to lock it into a trainee's long-term memory. Most of what happens over the period of the day will enter short-term memory and eventually be lost, but those events that are seen by the trainee as important will drift into long-term memory and be stored. Make sure that you vary the way in which the message is transmitted so that the chances of retention are greater.

Role plays The letters R O L E could well stand for Rehearsal Of Life Events, because role play sessions are meant to prepare people for situations that might happen. The role plays you use should be about situations that have happened in the past and are extremely likely to happen in the future. To prepare for this you should build up a series of case studies based on the combined experience of the salesforce. Take time to interview salespeople and managers about their experiences and build up some scripts and scenarios that will produce the ideal learning incident you are seeking to achieve. In the same way that the best books are usually those that have a basis of truth, the best role plays will also be based on real situations that have happened in the past. By sharing this information with trainees, you should also get a better level of acceptance from them.

Role plays and syndicate work are quite often used by trainers as a means of giving the group a break from stand-up trainers, but for most trainees are extremely boring. Watching other people role playing is a tedious affair and the monotony is only broken when your own turn arrives.

Training objective				
session	*methodology*	*notes*	*handouts*	*visuals*

Key	r=role play v=video camera d=discussion	s=syndicate c=case study f=film	q=quiz 	pp=personal presentation ft=formal test tl=trainer lecture

Figure 6.4   *Trainer's guide*

The problems associated with role play are typically trainer-induced. Lack of preparation and a low standard of professional execution means that the vast majority of role play situations do more harm than good. Preparing for a role play should be as demanding a job as producing a play, for many of the elements are the same. The more amateur your production the less effective will be the results. Here are some rules you should follow:

1 Use real case studies, not invented ones. These can be obtained from sales managers or even trainees.
2 Video people at least twice, in order to show some improvement.
3 Video everybody.
4 Let managers see the improvement, by showing results of your training on management development programmes.
5 Give written feedback to the trainee.
6 Let only trainers give feedback, not the trainees.
7 Allow time for rehearsal.
8 Make sure that the trainer/trainee ratio is not less than 1:4.
9 Make sure trainers are extremely competent in the use of video equipment.
10 Stop role plays as soon as they start going wrong. With recorded ones you can edit them.

Syndicates Setting small groups of people work tasks is a useful process in as much as it provides them with an opportunity to contribute to the training programme. It can also be ineffective and disruptive if not planned properly. Giving unclear instructions, setting the groups boring tasks, and not allowing sufficient feedback time, all contribute to potential disasters. You should also be aware of getting the construction of syndicates right. Some basic rules to follow are:

1 Keep numbers within a syndicate down to six and not less than three. Any more than six leads to endless discussion or some people withdrawing, and less than three just does not work.
2 Give clear instructions and check that the group knows what the task is by asking the syndicate leader to stand up and explain what they think they have to do. Elect the syndicate leader by pulling the name out of a hat. This avoids interminable negotiations. Keeping a record of who has spoken will ensure that everyone who wants to present is given the opportunity to do so, and those that do not are compelled to.
3 Allow plenty of time for each syndicate to present its work, and give encouraging feedback. It is important that syndicate members feel their efforts are acknowledged, otherwise any future syndicate work will be approached in a half-hearted manner.
4 Give the syndicate a meaningful exercise to do rather than some nonsense just to give the trainer a break. Announce a topic for discussion such as 'Replace the salesforce with computers' or some other contentious issue, and organize the feedback on a debate basis.
5 If possible, try to get each syndicate to feed back a different point. If you can set them different tasks in the first place this will help. Having a number of groups feeding back the same material can end up being boring and is unfair on the last group to present.
6 Make notes during the syndicate's presentation and summarize, giving positive feedback and stressing learning points.
7 Even though there is a group leader, make a point of asking other members of the team whether they feel their views have been aired. It is sometimes quite amusing to see how far the leader deviates from the originally agreed views.

Films Selecting the right films is difficult—you have to choose what is right for you and right for your particular company. Even though there is an enormous variety of films available, this does not mean you will find what you are looking for. Films I could recommend may not necessarily match the job profiles of your salespeople.

There is no easy way to choose a film. You have to see them and analyse what learning experiences you can develop from the film. Do not compromise. If only 10 per cent of the film is applicable to your company, do not use it. Even if 80 per cent is relevant, be aware of what the other 20 per cent is doing to your audience.

Do not use films simply as a leisure break—structure work before and after the film to reinforce its content. Showing films is a forceful learning medium but it can be abused.

Avoid films which more laughs than learning points. Humour helps, but there are some films that totally lose the message and simply provide a hilarious break from the task in hand. Sometimes it is better to select films with little or no humour and those that avoid using well-known actors. The latter can be distracting; if actors are extremely well-known, trainees tend to think about them in parts other than those being played out in the corporate video.

At some stage you will have to consider making your own films, using a professional agency. Their numbers are growing and the costs are decreasing. It is well worth allocating some of your budget to get exactly what you want rather than putting up with some generalized film that does not cover in detail what you need. Remember, the films on general release are made to cover as wide an audience as possible and, as a result, you pay for a watered-down version. Even though it may cost you twenty times as much to make a video than to buy one, the return on your investment will be substantially greater in the long run.

Quizzes

Using quizzes is a terrific way of making the learning process enjoyable and can reduce the tension in testing trainees' absorption of knowledge. Here are some ideas:

1 Split the group into teams and pick a group leader.
2 Organize your questions into individual and group questions. The group leader can decide who answers each question, but in any full quiz session a different person should answer each time.
3 Award five points for a correct individual answer, two points if the team has to answer, and three points if you have to pass it onto the next team to answer.
4 Announce the results after each round.
5 Get some prizes together such as sales books, cassettes or videos. They need not be expensive and indeed should not be. The quiz itself and the will to win will be sufficient to generate competition.
6 During the quiz introduce something like a 'joker' theme where each group can make a major presentation lasting no more than three minutes on any topic they choose at any time. The marks for this process are kept secret till the end of the session, and this heightens the enthusiasm with which the quiz is played.
7 Give marks indiscriminately for displays of positive attitudes, and even for smart ties. Take marks away for complaining and dirty shoes. Make it fun.

Structured sales process

Applying a structured approach to the sales process seems to have been with us for a long time (see page 63). The pages of many sales training magazines are full of proposed structures, each of which is sold as being unique. I see selling as a simple process, containing the elements of:

- Finding people
- Contacting people
- Selling yourself

all of which we shall examine in more detail later in this chapter.

By structured selling I mean following a rigid pattern, as prescribed by many trainers. My own research showed that 64 per cent of salespeople and sales managers feel that adopting a structured approach to selling should work and is desirable, and yet 57 per cent of salespeople said they found it difficult to put into practice. Sales managers that I questioned about what actually happened in the field said they saw little evidence of any structure being used by the vast majority of salespeople and certainly not by those salespeople who were successful. There is no evidence to support the practice of teaching salespeople a sales structure along the lines of:

- Presentation
- Handling objections
- Closing

In fact, more evidence exists that the practice of closing techniques is detrimental to the sales process rather than helpful, and we have already discussed the useless practice of concentrating on overcoming objections. So if the present use of concentrating on structured selling is pointless, what else is left?

The behavioural school

There is a strong school of thought that says that selling has more to do with personal relationships and behaviour than the learning of technique. I tend to favour this approach. It is a more professional approach but, unfortunately, far more difficult and time-consuming to embark upon. For this reason most trainers will go for the easy process of structured selling and closing techniques, both of which work on sales training courses, but have yet to be seen working successfully in the field.

Your greatest problem is to decide which behaviours you want to teach trainees, as many top salespeople do things naturally which they find difficult to explain and which are difficult to observe. In listening to many successful salespeople I was able to *feel* the difference, but putting it into words proved perplexing. It seems that successful salespeople act naturally and, indeed, I know a significant number of successful salespeople whose only common trait is that they are being themselves.

Robinson believes that salespeople are not very good at acting naturally and that the main purpose of role play training is to help salespeople identify their natural traits and use them to full advantage.

My own findings reinforce this view and that leads us to the problem of time and expense. The problem for managers and trainees alike is that this form of adaptive (or insight response) training is expensive. The single most cost-effective way of carrying this out, however, is by field coaching, although this means you will have to spend a considerable amount of energy in training managers. It may concern you that it will take some time before managers are competent enough to train their salespeople in the field, but even poor field coaching is better than no sales coaching at all. Salespeople have expectations about sales training. They believe that it will happen and that managers will deliver it in the field. When it does not happen their attitude towards all sales training suffers accordingly. This alone should lend greater importance to field coaching by line managers.

The debate about behaviour and whether it can be changed or not goes on. Perhaps the best that can be expected is a greater understanding of the effect that one's behaviour has on other people. My own view is that having been made aware of the effect of your behaviour on other people, that knowledge in itself changes your own behaviour, at least if you want it to.

I do think it is possible to change behaviour, given time and professional assistance. There are no easy answers because, as Weitz said, there are no universally effective sales behaviours. All sales jobs are different and even each sales situation is different. That means you have to teach salespeople to be flexible in their approach. This is possible by following the format shown in Figure 6.5

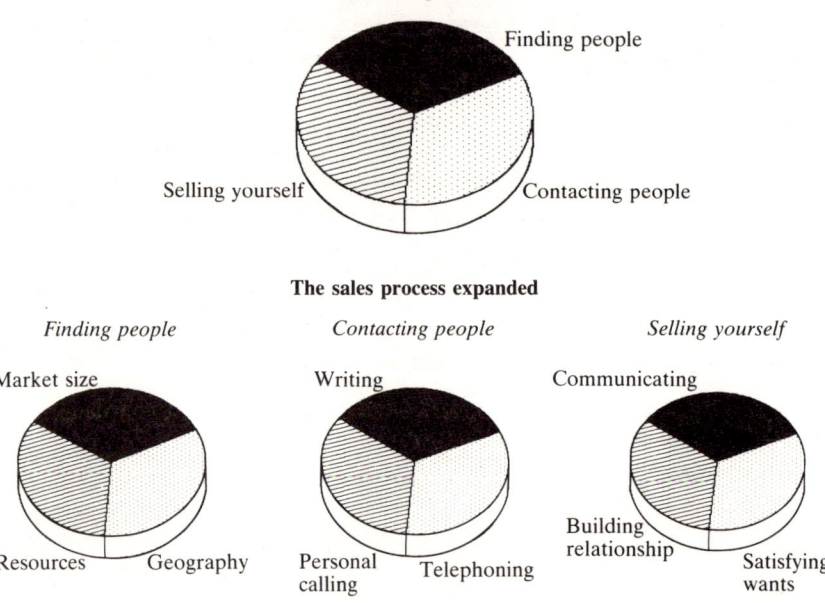

Figure 6.5   *A flexible approach to selling*

Finding people

Finding people is about determining the market size and the geography of the allocated area, and then using the available resources to approach customers. The most difficult thing salespeople have to do is find enough people to sell to, although successful salespeople find this relatively easy. So what is it that they do that unsuccessful salespeople do not? My belief is that successful salespeople are more aware of sales opportunities. All you can hope to achieve on a central training programme is to help salespeople understand where prospects are.

Either divide the group into syndicates or work on an individual basis and have them identify the size of the market and sources of business, the more the merrier. You may decide to help them by suggesting that the population can be split into gender; occupation; leisure groups; socio-economic groupings; age; district; or any other way you care to divide up the nearly sixty million people who live in Britain. Whichever way you look at it, prospecting is about realizing that the actual response you get from the total available market is significantly smaller than at first imagined. For this reason it has to be emphasized that prospecting is a continuous process. The best salespeople realize this and find that prospecting among existing customers is infinitely more rewarding than cold calling.

After a feedback session, have the lists that were produced written up and copied to the course. Make certain that you feed these lists back to line managers who can also use them in the field. If individuals back in the field have problems with identifying prospects the manager can refer them to the course content.

Beware of concentrating too much on prospecting. Paradoxically, I believe that prospecting plays the most significant role in salesperson success but it can also lead to salesperson failure. Spending an excessive amount of time in gathering information about prospects is pointless unless an approach is made.

Salespeople who are not confident, however, will absorb themselves in administrative tasks to the exclusion of prospect contact. Eric Berne says that this is known in transactional analysis terms as *withdrawal*. What this means is that people whose natural tendency is to avoid people contact will seek occupations and tasks that require little people contact but large amounts of solitude. You may say that these people do not exist in sales roles, but my research shows that trainers and managers create this problem through poor training and even poorer management.

A salesperson who is having a difficult time will use any method possible for showing that they are busy, while not actually selling. The easiest method is prospecting, or at least the effort required to collect possible prospects. They learn this process on training courses where too much emphasis is placed on how to collect information, and not enough on how easy it is and how dangerous it can be to spend too much time on the process.

Part of the training programme may be in making trainees aware of how to use the resources your company has. Obviously, this is determined by the size and structure of your company. You may have a marketing department that creates leads for salespeople, or at the very least supports your salesforce with advertising or direct mail campaigns. I believe that the more you do for your salespeople in terms of marketing support the less you need salespeople and hence the less the need for sales training. In many industries you hear the complaint from salespeople that if the company could find enough customers then the salesperson could concentrate on selling the company's products and services. They fail to realize that salespeople exist because the company cannot find enough people to buy its products and that is why they employ the most expensive distribution source imaginable – salespeople.

Contacting people

The most stressful part of a salesperson's job is the intial contact with the potential customer. Depending on what your company sells, initial contacts with customers can take any or all of the following forms:

- Writing
- Telephoning
- Personal calling

Writing

Like putting lists together, this is a potentially disastrous area for salespeople. The more time salespeople spend writing to customers the higher the chances are of sales failure. Like list-making, it can fool you into thinking that salespeople are busy.

Selling is more a 'doing' process and there are rarely good salespeople who can also write well. Producing good sales letters is an industry in itself and best left to professional writers. I recommend that your company produces as many standard letters as required and leaves the salesperson no other choice but to use them. If needed, make available in each sales office someone who can compose letters or, better still, install sufficient computerized word processing or expert systems to provide your salespeople with support. Over a number of years in direct selling, I have observed those whose days have been consumed with writing letters. They look busy. However, the really effective salesperson is usually poor at writing but good at verbal communication. It is up to you to decide what sort of sales job it is.

Telephoning

For many companies telephone selling represents their primary method of contacting customers and the industry of selling over the telephone grows daily. It is a highly specialized area and could form the basis of a book in its own right. I intend to tackle only the training requirements for teaching people how to obtain appointments using the telephone as part of the overall prospecting sequence and not the sales process itself.

The way in which we communicate with each other in a sales environment involves the use of the senses of sight, hearing and touch. Using the telephone to organize appointments presents us with the problem that the only tools at our disposal are words and tone of voice. This part of your training programme should, therefore, concentrate on *what* people say and, more importantly, on *how* they say it. As the sole emphasis here is on words and tone, I suggest you adopt a scripted approach and make trainees stick to it.

Before the training event, carry out some research and listen to successful salespeople to find out how they get their appointments and record their efforts. The only difficulty here is that successful salespeople will quite rapidly have established a network of customers and you will overhear them tapping into referred leads rather than cold canvassing. They rarely have to telephone people 'cold' because they get warm introductions from existing customers that make the telephone call sound far easier than it would be for a new trainee.

The successful salesperson and the sales manager, however, will be able to point you in the right direction and should quickly be able to provide you with a system that works for your business. The chances are that successful telephoning techniques will involve:

- considerable preparation in both materials and attitude
- the right environment in which to make telephone calls
- a script
- the use of alternatives, e.g. morning or afternoon? . . . Wednesday or Thursday?
- practice

Preparation   From researching your own company you will be able to determine with some certainty the likely problems that salespeople will encounter on the telephone. Most trainers will call these problems 'objections'. I prefer to call them sales opportunities. Customers rarely have objections to seeing other people who can benefit them. The problem they are faced with is that their experience is usually gained from listening to poorly trained and poorly managed salespeople who sound both unprofessional and ill-prepared to make telephone calls. The initial response of customers, therefore, is usually to say no. It's a reaction to past experience more than to current requests.

So the trainer's job is to make absolutely certain that salespeople understand that refusals are not aimed at them but at the past inadequate performance of poorly trained salespeople. If they follow the simple recipe that you will train them to use, they will be more successful than if they did not use it. I can guarantee that the following process works, but it is vital that trainees get plenty of time to practise, both on the central course and in the field. All managers in the company must be able to coach salespeople in the same way and stick to the format, no matter how long it takes an individual to acquire the skill. Even using this system, rejection can occur in large doses, and the natural tendency is then to give up and try something else. Any newly learned skill involves a period of settling in when performance can initially deteriorate. The longer-term results, however, are always a substantial increase in performance.

Using the simple form shown in Figure 6.6, get groups of trainees to come up with as many reasons as they think customers might give for not agreeing to an appointment. Good preparation on your part will ensure that trainees will never come up with reasons you have not heard before and, therefore, cannot answer. When the group attempts to answer these refusals you should be able to help when necessary without reference to your notes.

do this in pairs

When sufficient time has been allowed to think up refusals, swap papers among the groups so that one group is attempting to answer the reasons thought up by another. You can then use the same process in the feedback session as for quizzes by awarding points for good responses, and generally making the feedback session enjoyable and stimulating. This practice works well and relieves the tension most salespeople feel about using the telephone.

This session can take some time, but it is important you cover every problem that comes up and that each reason is given a suitable answer. You should not progress to the next stage leaving any requests unanswered. Everyone should feel comfortable and confident that no matter what the reason given an answer is available.

Quote. ←——

That is not to say that in reality appointments will be achieved every time. In some industries less than 10 per cent of telephone calls may result in an appointment. The important thing is to have a sufficiently large pool of potential customers to telephone.

Type of refusal	Possible answer

Figure 6.6 *Format for dealing with telephone refusals*

Environment Much can be said about making telephone calls in the right sort of environment, such as a quiet room with no distractions. Yet there are telesales organizations that do tremendously well by having people make their telephone calls in front of their peers, who encourage them to success. I believe that basic common sense dictates the rules here. People should be mentally well prepared to make the telephone call in the first place and address the event in a professional manner. This involves smiling down the telephone, speaking clearly and slowly, and not smoking or drinking coffee while making calls. This might seem obvious, but it is surprising how few salespeople consider these elementary points.

For me, there are two basic requirements for successful telephone selling of appointments:

1 Trainees must be shown the importance of standing up when making telephone calls. In most cases, before training, trainees will take and make telephone calls sitting down. While sitting down, looking at papers on the desk, and speaking into a telephone, the natural body posture is one of a hunched back and hence a concave chest. This restricts breathing which is compounded by the stress of the sales process. Within a couple of calls it is not unusual for all calls to sound lack-lustre and boring. The effect of standing up to make calls is and sounds dramatic. Breathing is easier, the standing position is more dominant, and continuous telephoning is no problem.
2 They must have all the tools to hand, such as a script, diary and a pen that works, with a back-up if it runs dry.

The only way to train people how to use the telephone is to arrange to have dummy telephones available for role play. Wherever possible the trainer should play the part of the customer. Trainees telephoning each other can defeat the object, as they tend either to be too nice to each other or to reduce the event to the farcical. As telephone sales training can be a tense affair, trainees will quite quickly respond to the first attempt at humour in the session, and you could lose many of the learning points you are trying to achieve.

Record on cassette and video tape a number of attempts before showing them how it should be done. Record the second attempt after training and the improvement should be self-evident.

The format for a successful telephone sales call seeking an appointment is as follows:

1 Have all the material needed to make the call within easy sight and placed in such a way as to avoid having to rummage through documents or paperwork to conclude the call.

Quote

2 The only purpose of the call is to get an appointment. Trainees should understand that they are telephoning the client to establish *when* to make the appointment, not *whether* to make an appointment.
3 Stand up to make telephone calls.

4 State clearly and precisely name, company and purpose of call—which is to make an appointment.
5 Give alternative times for the appointment (i.e. Monday or Friday; morning or afternoon; this week or next week; nine o'clock or ten o'clock).
6 Repeat the arranged time, confirm the address and say goodbye.

Using a script   The effective way to teach people how to sell on the telephone is to use a script. It can be put into the format shown in Figure 6.7 and, if needed, can be read off while making a telephone call. Trainees may resist using a script and say that it does not sound natural. They could be right. However, practice makes perfect. You may be surprised how many company helplines are staffed by people reading from a script which appears on a computer screen. In fact, the better the response you get on the telephone the higher the chance that the salesperson at the other end has been trained to use a script. The falseness and discomfort will soon disappear as trainees practise.

Each person should be allowed to practise on the telephone until such time as they are able to answer all problem calls without reference to a script. You could arrange for people to work in teams, and award a small prize for the first team that helps all its members to achieve the

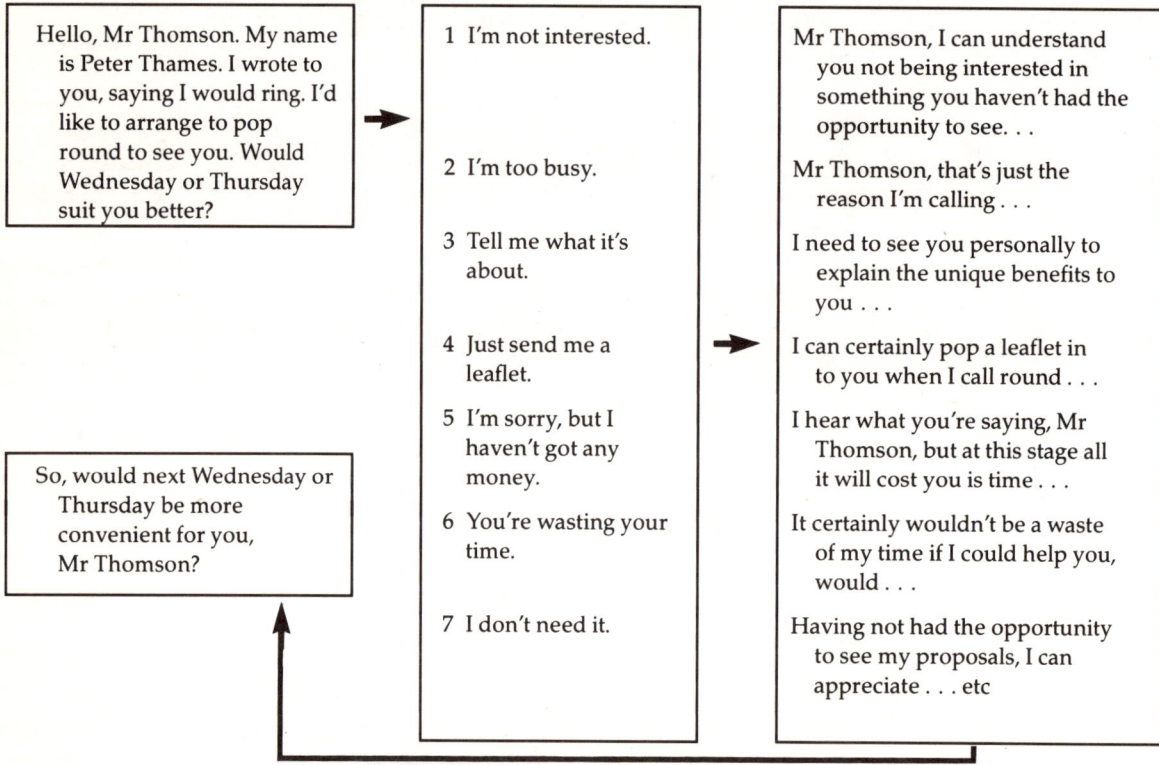

Figure 6.7   *Telephone script*

goal of making successful calls without reference to a script. Although it may be difficult, try not to finish this event until all teams have successfully completed the task. You could still be working at midnight!

Personal calling

The quickest way of establishing contacts with customers is to call and see them without an appointment. Many salespeople find this the most productive method, and it certainly saves on the paperwork and the telephone bills. It does, however, take a great deal of confidence and the ability to accept rejection.

If you want to encourage this sort of canvassing it will mean a considerable amount of time helping trainees to practise cold calling so that they feel confident about it.

There is no secret to cold calling or training people to cold call other than repetition. You could write a script for trainees to learn and follow, or simply let them make up an introduction themselves. It doesn't really matter what they say—the success comes from *how* they say it. Confidence in cold calling comes from practice, perseverance and a positive attitude. Your simple job as a trainer is to allow people to make all their mistakes in the training room so that they get it right in the field.

We regularly have salespeople calling on us, selling anything from alarm systems to double glazing. I'm not in the market for either, but if I was I would buy from those few young bloods I see who have learned their scripts well and have obviously practised. Like other salespeople, I am probably easier to sell to than most other people. I do, however, react badly to poorly prepared salespeople. It's not them I blame, so much as their managers and their trainers.

There are some easier forms of personal contacts that you could encourage salespeople to develop and these concern people that the trainee already knows. It really does not matter who trainees know, or who they are related to, or live next door to, the chances are high that they must know somebody who could buy the company's products, or at the very least introduce them to someone else who could. Salespeople constantly complain that companies do not provide them with sufficient leads and yet their own environments are filled with leads.

Using the following format, have trainees answer the questions individually and then discuss in the group. Your aim is to show trainees that business exists everywhere—all they have to do is look.

Prospecting

1 How many people are there in your family?
2 Write down the names of the firms you can remember where your relatives work.
3 How many friends do you think each of your relatives has?
4 How many firms do you think they work at?
5 How many friends do you know?

6 How many neighbours do you know?

7 How many casual acquaintances do you have?

8 How many companies do you think the people in questions 5, 6 and 7 work at?

9 What do you do in your leisure time that involves meeting other people?

10 How many people?

11 How many clubs and associations are there in your area? If you do not know, how can you find out?

12 How many people—colleagues, customers and suppliers—did you come into contact with in your last job?

13 How many entries are there in your local telephone directory?

14 What is the population of the place where you live?

15 How many houses are within one hour's walking distance of your home?

16 How many companies have premises within a five-mile radius of your home?

17 How many local papers, including 'frees', are there in your area?

18 Have you ever thought about how many people shop in the same place as you do?

19 How many people live in your region?

20 How many people live in the UK?

Following this exercise it is back to practising introductions to friends, neighbours and relatives.

Selling yourself

The focus of personal sales training is selling yourself. Selling yourself involves communicating, satisfying wants and building relationships (see Figure 6.5). If the sales training you deliver involves the process of successfully selling yourself then you will have achieved a great deal. The purpose of the central sales training programme is to give salespeople the best possible start to their sales jobs. It then rests with managers to complement that training in the field, and we shall see in the next chapter how they should discharge that duty.

Selling yourself is something that happens within the first few minutes of a sales call in any market. In some types of sales jobs a large number of calls may be involved but the success of any relationship can be traced back to the first few minutes of meeting a new prospect. It is within the first few minutes of a sales call that a potential customer will decide whether a salesperson has anything worth listening to in both the short and long term. Your job is to help salespeople realize this, and to prepare them to present their sales story in the best possible light, as quickly as possible.

Body language

We have already discussed body language and I can only reiterate its importance in the sales process. You must decide what resources you have available to devote to the subject. My own feeling is that the more you spend on training your salespeople to recognize and use body language the more successful will be their communication with customers. Again, the problem is that body language training involves time, which in many companies is a scarce commodity. You can only hope to scratch the surface on a central course and should, therefore, make sure that you train your managers in greater depth so that when they are training their salespeople in the field they can build on the work you have done in the classroom.

This is not the place to cover the subject of body language in detail, so I have included suggested reading and reference material at the end of this chapter. The important thing to remember about body language is that, faced with a message in verbal and non-verbal forms, people will always accept the non-verbal message more easily than the verbal message. Also, if conflict exists between what is being said and what is being displayed in body language signals, people will believe what the body is saying and not what the words mean. For this reason, if you intend to use scripts to teach your salespeople, it can be a waste of time if trainees are not also taught *how* to say the words.

Included in body language training should also be a section on image. You must decide what sort of image you are trying to portray as a company and then match that with the people you recruit. Your problem is that selection processes are not always very good at spotting the professional candidates. Some people can look totally different during the selection process from the way they eventually behave on training courses. By the time they get out into the field you could be forgiven for believing that some form of metamorphosis has taken place.

The most effective way to make the point about image is to ask individual trainees to make a short presentation on what they believe customer expectations might be of them, as salespeople. Use the format shown in Figure 6.8.

Satisfying wants   People buy products and services for what they do, not what they are. Also, there is a great tendency for people to buy what they *want* and not what they *need*. Quickly dealing with the second point first, ask trainees to write down how many shirts/blouses they have in their wardrobes at home. Then ask a similar question about shoes, trousers and skirts. Now ask them how many of these things they need. The point is that people buy what they want and not what they need.

Marketing convinces us that people buy what they need and the function of marketing is to produce the products and services that people need. If that were only true, we would not need salespeople. Fortunately, it is one of those myths of the twentieth century business environment that has little validity and we find we still need salespeople to sell customers what they want. To persuade customers to buy what they want, however, salespeople have to present their products and services in such a way that customers can make a choice. Customers can only make a

---

Customer Perceptions

Make a two-minute presentation which incorporates answers to as many of the following questions as possible:

1 What will prospective customers expect to see when you turn up?
2 What should your clothes look like?
3 What should your hair look like?
4 What effect, if any, will your shape have on customers?
5 If your customer does not smoke, will they know that you do, and would it make any difference?
6 What should the things that you bring with you to your meeting look like?
7 What will the customer expect to hear?
8 What should your voice sound like?
9 What things could you do with your voice, speech and presentation that would distract or even annoy your customer?
10 How do you want your prospective customers to feel?
11 How do you intend to achieve all this?

Figure 6.8 *Creating an image*

choice if they have sufficient information in an understandable format to make what they feel is the correct decision. This all seems so obvious that I am constantly surprised how many people quite simply miss the whole point of personal selling. The rules are simple:

1 Find out what people want.
2 Give it to them.

This simplicity, however, seems to cause confusion in the sales training industry. I am often asked why more people don't do it, if it is that simple. The answer is that it is better to make it complicated and difficult so that there is plenty of money to be made training people how to do something that is perceived to be impossible. I find it impossible to make selling complicated. Let's look at the rules again:

1 Find out what people want.
2 Give it to them.

I concede that there are possibly another two items:

1 Before salespeople can find out what people want, they must be able to display common communication attributes which enable prospective clients to feel comfortable in examining alternatives.
2 Everything that we want has a price attached to it. In sales transactions between customer and salesperson this could involve charging a fee, commission or a price.

This, in turn, means that salespeople should be confident about the products or services they are selling. This may seem obvious, but with many salespeople there seems to be a resistance to charging a fee for

services or some shame attached to earning commissions. In many ways, salespeople are generally happier if no money is involved in customer transactions. Most salespeople are looking to work for the company that has the best products at the lowest price. The search is as elusive as finding the investment vehicle that produces the highest return with no risk. This stops neither investors nor salespeople from continuing the exploration.

Much of this has to do with confidence which we will cover later in this chapter.

To help salespeople establish a method for helping customers to find out what they want, you have to train salespeople to understand their own company products and services in customer jargon. Customers speak in benefits, salespeople speak in features.

Features and benefits
Customers are only interested in what products will do for them, not what products are. You have to get salespeople to paint word pictures for people.

Salespeople are usually very good at identifying the main characteristics of products or services that the company offers. Use the form shown in Figure 6.9 for any type of product or service, getting trainees to identify for each separate product the main characteristics and corresponding benefits for the customer or prospect. Use a similar process to that suggested earlier for the telephone sales exercise—creating teams, awarding points, and fostering competition. Then have individuals or teams feed back their findings, introducing a third element into the proceeding; read out the product feature and use a joining benefit statement from the following list to explain what it does for the prospect:

- What this means is . . .
- Put another way . . .
- That means . . .
- The benefit to you is . . .
- If I can explain the benefit to you . . .
- Putting that differently . . .

You can develop many other ways of expressing the same link. You are seeking to have trainees describe the company's products in the following way:

- This new computer has a 386 processor, and what this means for you is that you can process your work in half the time it takes you to do it now.
- This policy includes a waiver of premium, which means that if you fall ill and can't pay, then the insurance company will not cancel the policy.
- The price of the new chocolate bar has been increased but so has the size, and the benefit to you will be increased turnover.
- You will get a refund if anything goes wrong, in other words you will still be able to enjoy that holiday of a lifetime.

Product name or service:	
Main characteristics or features	*What does it do for the prospect?*

Figure 6.9　*Breaking down product and service features into customer benefits*

A large part of your course should be devoted to this process. It does not come easy to salespeople, especially those with experience who have learned bad selling habits.

Confidence

and the.

Personal selling is laden with rejection from the initial contact to finally asking for the order. One of the greatest problems faced by trainers and managers of salespeople is that most salespeople are more frightened of failing than they are determined to succeed. For this reason, most salespeople tend to act quite differently with prospects from the way they do with people they know. You should explain to them that with people they know they tend not to feel uncomfortable because they sold themselves to those people some time ago. The problem with new people is that it takes some time to get to know them, to break the ice, but that it is vital as a salesperson that they are able to do this. It is only from getting to know their customers over a period of time that they build long-term relationships, and it is the long-term relationship that reaps the most financial rewards.

What makes a successful consultant

Ask trainees, individually, to write down the characteristics of a successful salesperson. I can guarantee that everyone will have the word 'confidence' in their list and this is the word you are looking for. Write up their lists on a flip-chart and discuss all the characteristics, asking trainees to explain what they mean by them. Leave confidence to the last.

Take some time now to develop a discussion about what they really mean by the word 'confident'. Introduce questions such as:

- Are salespeople successful because they are confident, or are they confident because they are successful—which comes first?

- What are successful salespeople confident about?
- Name some confident people who are not successful.
- Name a character in a play, or a film, that you have seen recently who epitomized confidence.

The next question is important and should be handled carefully.

- Was the character real or did the actor make them seem real? Obviously a good actor brings a part alive, and makes the fictional character seem real.

The point to make is that by acting confidently, others will endow you with confidence.

Using the following format, have trainees list the benefits of their company, their products and themselves to their customers.

USP list ——▷

Benefits

1 List as many benefits of your company that you can think of.
2 List as many benefits that your products and services have for customers that you can think of.
3 What benefits do you as an individual bring (a) to your company, and (b) to your customers?

You should then spend a considerable amount of time encouraging trainees to make short presentations to the group, feeding back their answers.

Asking questions

I don't think I have been on a sales course without the subject of open questions and closed questions coming up. Closed questions are supposed to be those that will result in a one-word answer, and usually give customers the opportunity to say no. By asking the magic open-ended questions that begin with 'How', 'Why', 'Where', 'What', 'When' and 'Who', riches beyond imagination will be yours. I once read a research paper on open-ended and closed questions and became more confused than before I started. I have asked closed questions and people bought from me, and open questions and people did not want to talk. I have said nothing and people have opened up. If there was such a thing as open-ended questions then life would certainly be a lot easier for salespeople. They work on sales courses, as most things do, and trainees quickly learn to play the training game. In life, out in the field, good salespeople couldn't tell you the difference. It is not what they say that matters, it is *how* they say it.

Open question

For example, how many different ways are there of saying 'I did not say that you told a lie'? I counted five—how many did you come up with?

I can go home and in passing say 'Had a busy day?' Depending on *how* I say it, and how my wife hears it, this comment alone, can have a multitude of outcomes.

Words mean very little. That's part of the problem with this book. I write in my voice, attaching a meaning to the words I write, and you read in your voice, attaching, perhaps, a different meaning. If we are lucky, we will come close to some understanding, but it is not guaranteed.

If I say to you 'This is no criticism of you personally', would you believe me?

It is not the *type* of question that matters, but the way in which the question is asked. All successful salespeople are good at asking questions. It comes naturally to them, or so it would seem, and yet the only way to learn the skill is to practise it constantly.

Taking the benefit statements that we looked at earlier, the only thing missing from them, and the thing that will turn the statement into a buying situation, is a question at the end of the statement:

- This policy includes a waiver of premium, which means that if you fall ill and are not able to pay, then the insurance company will not cancel the policy. That seems like a good idea, doesn't it?
- This new computer has a 386 processor, and what this means for you is that you can process your work in half the time it takes you to do it now. That has to be a real benefit, hasn't it?
- The price of the new chocolate bar has been increased but so has the size, and the benefit to you will be increased turnover. I suppose that would not go amiss, would it?
- You will get a refund if anything goes wrong, in other words you will still be able to enjoy that holiday of a lifetime. That is what you want, isn't it?

You can have great fun developing this sort of questioning technique. There are no short cuts, however. Make trainees practise all day if necessary so that they appear to be asking these sort of questions naturally.

After this, you could get them to play around with the statements by putting the question elsewhere in the sales statement or simply by rephrasing the statements so that they sound like questions:

- If I could show you a way to protect the policy in case you are not able to pay the premiums, you would be interested, wouldn't you?
- That holiday is important to you, I know that, and making sure that nothing interferes with your taking it is vital, isn't it?
- I guess that anything that can help you to increase turnover must be of interest to you? (This does not even look like a question, but it can be made to sound like one.)
- Most people would like to do their work in half the time, and you are no different, are you? So if I was to show you something that could do that for you, you'd be interested? (In this case 'wouldn't you?' is implied but left out.)

Key points

1 The central training department has two important functions: training sales managers to train, and providing foundation sales training for new starters.

2 Selling skills are difficult to acquire and take considerable time, effort and practice.

3 Selling is an emotional skill.

4 Sales managers are coaches.

5 Managers and trainees should realize that performance can suffer initially when learning a new skill. It is imperative to keep practising the new skill until performance improves.

6 A great deal of learning can be achieved through self-study.

7 The training venue is important, and the company should invest in its own training premises to show it is serious about training. With your own venue it becomes easier to control all aspects of the training event.

8 Training events should not be an endurance course. Have plenty of breaks and a schedule flexible enough to cater for a variety of learning speeds. The trainer's notes are a guide only and not a rigid format.

9 Use a full range of training techniques on training events to stimulate learning and aid retention.

10 Selling is a three-part process: finding people; contacting people; and selling yourself. The most difficult part of the process for salespeople is finding enough people to sell to. The most important part of the process is selling yourself.

11 The rules of personal selling are simple enough: find out what people want, and let them have it.

12 A large part of any sales course involves teaching trainees to convert product features and services into understandable customer benefits. This is easy to do on courses, but salespeople find it difficult to do in the field.

13 Successful salespeople are confident. Trainers have to create an environment in which trainees can build confidence in their attributes and in their company.

14 An integral part of successful selling is the ability to ask the right type of questions, in the right way.

Recommended reading

Atkinson, R.L., E.C. Atkinson and E.R. Hilgard, *Introduction to Psychology*, Harcourt Brace Jovanovich 1981.

Barker, D. *TA and Training: The theory and use of transactional analysis in organisations*, Gower 1980.

Berne, E. *A Layman's Guide to Psychiatry and Psychoanalysis*, Penguin 1971.

Blacker F. and S. Shimmin, *Applying Psychology in Organisations*, Methuen 1984.

Clark, N. *Managing Personal Learning and Change: a trainer's guide*, McGraw-Hill 1990.

Hopkins, T. *How to Master the Art of Selling*, Tom Hopkins International 1982.

Jacoby J. and C. Craig (eds) *Personal selling: theory, research, and practice*, Lexington Books 1984.

Leeds, D. *Powerspeak: the complete guide to public speaking and presentation*, Piatkus 1988.

McKenna, E. *Psychology in Business*, Lawrence Erlbaum Associates Ltd 1987.

Morrison, J.H. and J.J. O'Herne, *Practical transactional analysis in management*, Addison Wesley 1977.

Rae, L. *The Skills of Human Relations Training*, Gower 1985.

Spooncer, F. *Behavioural Studies for Marketing and Business*, Hutchinson Education 1989.

Tanner, D. *That's not what I meant! How conversational style makes or breaks your relationships with others*, J.M. Dent & Sons Ltd 1986.

References

Berne, E. *Games People Play*, Penguin 1967.

Robinson, L.B. 'Role playing as a sales training tool', *Harvard Business Review* May/June 1987.

Weitz, B.A. 'Effectiveness in sales interactions', *Journal of Marketing* 1981.

7 The field training programme

This chapter aims to answer the following questions:

- What are the components of a field training programme?
- What part does field training play in overall sales success?
- What role do sales meetings have in the overall training plan?

Field training

A major function of field training is to reinforce what has already been taught on a central course. The influence of the sales manager here is crucial. Sales managers will very quickly confirm the validity of all past and future training initiatives that the company embarks upon by their actions immediately following the central training event. Your aim is for consistency of approach so that trainees understand what is required of them in the acquisition of knowledge and the execution of newly learned skills. The only person who can effectively communicate this is the sales manager. The problem is that many sales managers are completely unaware of their power and influence.

I once asked a national sales manager to speak to a group of new trainees. He asked me what he should say and was shocked to hear me reply: 'Say what you like, but whatever you say, understand that they will hang on every word and believe whatever you say'.

The way in which the sales manager communicates with a trainee following a sales course involves the same rules that apply to all sales situations. New trainees are trying to sell themselves to the sales manager. Selling is a precarious profession and for many salespeople their existence relies heavily on currying favour with sales managers. Salespeople are expected to perform immediately but in reality this is an extremely unrealistic objective. In the early days of a new sales career, therefore, salespeople are very conscious of their vulnerability and try desperately to earn approval to give themselves a feeling of security. In these initial stages, they hang on every word and action of the sales manager. So sales managers need to understand the communication process, especially with regard to their own behaviour, and this is one of the reasons for putting sales managers through the sames sales training as salespeople.

We have already seen the importance of body language in communication. Just because the sales manager asks the trainee 'How did the course go?' it doesn't convey that he is interested or even cares if at the same time he is fingering his pen, hovering over a desk full of papers, and sounding totally uninterested. The question itself is rather pointless and perhaps even shows the manager's lack of expectations of the course. Far better to train your sales managers to say something like:

I know that the course you have just been on will have prepared you for an extremely successful career, and I feel very confident that this major investment in your training will pay enormous dividends. My job now is to build on that process and I want to discuss with you how we can transfer that learning into practical application on the job.

While saying this the sales manager must sound enthusiastic, and act enthusiastically. He does this by clearing his desk of other work, stopping all calls to his office, and sitting next to the trainee so that his body language signals will clearly convey his interest and attention.

The field visit

As soon as possible after the central training event, the sales manager should accompany the new salesperson in the field. Ideally, new salespeople must not be allowed to make their first call unaccompanied. If you allow them to make mistakes and learn bad habits in the first week of their job, it will take you a lifetime to alter them.

Some companies adopt the 'sitting with nelly' approach to training salespeople and send new starters out with existing salespeople. Sometimes it works, most times it doesn't. It is the manager's responsibility to train new salespeople as well as existing salespeople.

Sales training in the field involves the four elements shown in Figure 7.1:

- Setting objectives
- Observation
- Giving feedback
- Demonstration

Surprisingly few sales managers have any idea why they carry out field visits with salespeople, other than that is something they have to be seen to do; it is highly likely to be something they do not enjoy doing. Managers, in my experience, undergo some form of metamorphosis during the time it takes to change from a salesperson to a manager. In the latter stages of this change, and the time scales are from Friday night to Monday morning, managers believe that great wisdom is bestowed upon them, relieving them of the necessity to sell ever again.

The single most important message that you must seek agreement on is that:

Managers are coaches

Together with the managing director you should design a formal process for field visits that revolves around a structured training event. The MD must be seen to be involved in this process to give it credibility and

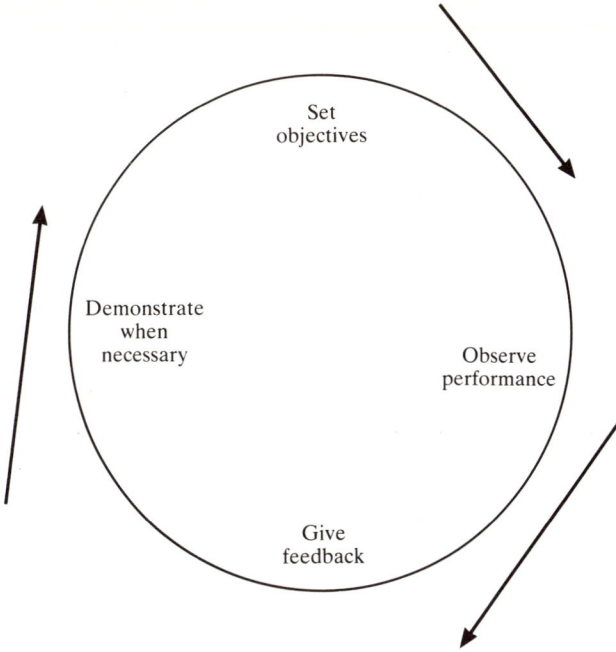

Figure 7.1   *Field training*

also to force unwilling sales managers to carry out their most important role—that of coaching their salespeople. The MD also needs to reinforce this message by examining the effectiveness of field visits. You can help him to to this by instigating a formal procedure for field visits in the format like the one that follows.

Field visit programme

The field visit should be seen as part of a formal training, development and appraisal system. I have taken it for granted that your company has an appraisal system. If not you must introduce one immediately. If your company does not have an appraisal system then it does not believe in developing people.

Having a formal field training system is all part of creating a Level One training department. In the early days you could meet with significant resistance from sales managers in producing regular field training reports and keeping training logs for all their team. At the outset the task may seem onerous, so you need to ensure, first, that the system is simple and, second, that managers, especially the national sales manager, receive plenty of feedback.

In reality, there are only a few simple items that you as a trainer, and your colleagues as line managers, should be interested in:

1 Have trainees understood the content of the central training programme and are they able to see its relevance to the job?
2 Do managers agree with the contents of the central training programme and can they continue the same process in the field?
3 Does what has been taught on the central training programme work?

Field Visit Form
Salesperson: Sales Manager:
Date: Number of calls: Type:
Purpose of field visit:
Observations:
Action points for next field visit:
Signature: Signature:

Figure 7.2   *Field visit report form*

This is where managers make or break the effort expended on the central programme. Whatever happens, the message from field training must reinforce the messages given on the central programme. In the early days of learning a new skill many trainees will be desperately seeking for a message from the manager along the lines of:

'Don't worry, it's not you. That system of selling they told you about on the course doesn't work in real life. I'll show you how to do it.'

If this is indeed the case, then change the system on the central course, but whatever you do make certain that central training and field training are compatible. The only way you can achieve this is to introduce a formal system of reporting. It is up to you to design a system suitable for your own company, but a suggested format is shown in Figure 7.2.

Setting objectives   The purpose of the field visit should be clearly understood by both parties. It is not sufficient to say that the purpose of a field training day is to increase sales—that in itself is obvious and need not be written down. Salespeople are not so stupid as to fail to understand the necessity to increase sales. Sales, however, are made up of a number of aspects, and it is the job of a sales manager to determine how best to approach a field training programme by concentrating on one area of the sales process at a time. It should be realized that it is unrealistic to expect to put everything right on one visit. The first visit might just be one of observation, and this in itself could be the sole objective of the day.

A good athletic coach knows that it is impossible to improve all aspects of performance in one go. A coach told me: 'The object of a coach is to observe a total performance and pick out those areas of skill that will contribute to increased performance. This means dealing with one thing at a time. Trying to enhance someone's total skills is difficult. If you cover too much too quickly, you dishearten the athlete and they give up. Think of it in terms of whole—part—whole. You observe the whole performance, then pick a part of it, improve it, and watch the effect it then has on the whole performance'.

Managers need to be advised to concentrate on only one area per field day. The reason most managers try to cover too much on field visits is that field visits are infrequent and too short. Managers then try to justify their existence by covering too much information in too short a period and in the process confuse the trainee.

The sort of objectives that could be set are:

- To examine the way in which the first few minutes of the sales call are handled, and the way in which the salesperson explains to the customer the purpose of the call.
- To help the salesperson recognize customers' body language signals and to take appropriate action.
- To coach the salesperson in offering alternative times when seeking appointments using the telephone.
- To develop the skill of explaining company products without the use of jargon.

Obviously, as a field training programme is built up, the objectives could also include a review of previous training sessions and their application in the field. This follow-up can include the results of formal classroom training delivered during sales meetings:

- To examine the practical application of agreed phrases practised at the last sales meeting.
- To check that the questions learned on the last field visit are now being used.

Using objective setting in this way, field training can be seen to have practical application for salespeople, be relevant to their jobs, and be part of a total development programme. The last point is important. Salespeople should feel that training is continuous and a field training programme is a visible example of the company's commitment to continuous development. Unless a system like this is operated then you will find it impossible to rid the company of what I call 'courseitis', a complaint that infects many companies and involves them in costly training events which quite simply do not work.

A field training day should be for a whole day. Agree with the national sales manager that a field training day should never be less than one full day. What managers hope to achieve in less than that time eludes me but I can guarantee that 90 per cent of sales managers throughout the country spend considerably less time than that with their salespeople, if they manage to spend any time with them at all.

Observation

The one thing managers hate doing is observing salespeople. Many managers see their job as proving to the salesperson how good they are at selling. Managers are coaches, but coaching should be at the end of the chain of a field visit programme. Before coaching a salesperson to sell, managers have to discover the salesperson's shortcomings. The only way that this can be achieved is to watch the salesperson over a number of calls, without commenting, and then review at the end of a full day. It is impossible to formulate a rational picture of a salesperson's competence without an extended observation period. It is doubtful whether one day is sufficient, as it takes little account of having an 'off' day, but at least it would be a significant start.

The field training programme has to be seen as a continuous affair, and it is unrealistic to assume that problems can be identified and solved in one visit. It would probably be a good idea to have a field training event cover two days—one day to observe and the second to correct any problems. You will probably find sales managers saying they have not got the time to spend two days with one salesperpson. What about the paperwork, what about the meetings, what about the rest of the team and their needs?

You should constantly return to the agreed policy that managers are coaches. If managers are constantly involved in other activities that eat up their time, get rid of the things that get in the way of field coaching. If you want managers to administrate then employ administrators not sales managers. Companies seem to insist on making a manager's job so diverse that probably only 2 per cent of the managerial population could effectively do the job in the first place. Ask yourself regularly: 'What is the main purpose of the sales manager?' If the answer is that the manager is responsible for getting results through other people, then understand that coping with administrative details and attending meetings will not get things done through other people. If it costs a fortune to introduce a computerized system of adminstration, then do it.

During a sales call, the primary function of the sales manager is to shut up. It is extremely difficult to observe clearly and remember what is going on during a sales presentation. It is impossible to observe properly or remember anything if the sales manager is involved in the sales process. Many managers feel uncomfortable about taking part in sales calls and saying nothing, but it really depends on how the accompanied call is sold to the customer in the first place.

The usual practice is to say that the manager is a colleague or a trainee. This lie is spotted by all customers. In the customer's mind the colleague is clearly more confident than the salesperson. Before long the customer is talking all the time to the manager and the salesperson has learned very little other than how not to manage and motivate salespeople. Managers have said to me that if they introduce themselves as the manager then this scenario will ensue. This is not true. The way in which managers introduce themselves could be along the lines of:

I am John's manager. The reason I am here today is to observe the sort of service that we give to an important customer like yourself in order that we as a company can constantly improve. If it's all right with you I would like to take part in this call by merely observing. Is that all right?

In my first sales management role I used to accompany salespeople on calls to department stores, supermarkets, newsagents and the like, delivering books and merchandizing book displays. So as not to interfere with the sales process I would walk away, peeking at the sale from behind a gondola or a book stand. It made me feel stupid, unnerved the salesperson, amused the customer, and I missed half of what was going on. Next call I tried introducing myself as a trainee, only to be told 'I thought you were the area sales manager'. Eventually, and since then, I have introduced myself in the above format and it has never produced any problems. It lets all parties know what the game is and what everyone's role is. In many ways customers feel flattered that companies bother.

Giving feedback

You must spend time training sales managers how to give feedback. Left to their own devices they ask inane questions like:

• So, how do you think that call went?

Salespeople understand the field visit game and say:

• I thought it was all right, what do you think?

Feedback should only be given at the end of a full day's calls. It should be explained that the manager will not comment on each individual call, but will seek to build up a total picture of the full day, concentrating only on the agreed primary objectives. That does not stop both parties entering into discussion over other items that may have come up, but it is really important to match the feedback with the objective of the day.

It would be unrealistic to cover other items because managers should not be taking notes during sales presentations. After each call, on the way to the next call, is the ideal opportunity for managers to gather their thoughts together and prepare for the end-of-the-day feedback.

The manager should also be aware how uncomfortable criticism is, even when prefaced by: 'This is no criticism of you personally, but . . .'. The manager must make the trainee feel comfortable about feedback and its purpose in the salesperson's total development programme:

John, both of us understand that having a manager with you on a day's training can potentially be distracting and, obviously, I take that very much into account. The purpose of today was to examine in detail the area you were experiencing difficulty with last time and that was . . .

It is then vital that feedback begins with good news, even if there isn't any. It could be that the only good thing about the day was shiny shoes, but whatever it is sales managers should be taught to give good news first. Much of what managers have to deal with, day to day, involves problems and they develop an immunity to receiving and giving bad news. They tend to forget that just as many good things happen in any one day, as bad.

During your training of sales managers, have them pair off and arrange the seating so that two managers sit facing each other. Ask them to say nice things about the manager opposite. This feedback should include something about why they either admire or like the manager and they have to tell them this face to face. Believe me, they will find it difficult, especially saying it with a straight face. Swap managers around until you are happy that they are able to face each other, say good things about their colleagues direct to their face without laughing, and also understand what it is like to receive good feedback.

Salespeople want to be liked, and it is the manager's job to help them feel good about themselves. That's not to say they have to hide the bad things, but feedback should be on a sandwich basis—say something good, fill the sandwich with those items that need discussing, and end up with praise. Good news, bad news, good news.

One manager I explained this system to came back to me a few months later and said: 'Frank, that sandwich thing really works. I was out with someone yesterday and after the call I said to him, "Peter, that was probably the best sales call you've ever done. The problem is it isn't good enough, so you're fired. By the way, that's a nice tie you're wearing".'

Demonstration

One of the most positive things a manager can do for trainees is show them how to sell. It needs to be handled carefully however. Managers should not set out to prove they are better than their salespeople, but merely to show them that they are managers because they can sell, continue to know how to sell, and are taking the role of coach. It is for this reason that only salespeople can be sales managers. In showing salespeople how to sell, managers may very well produce salespeople who become far better than they are, and that's the whole point. The manager's job is to get salespeople to sell a far greater quantity than managers could on their own.

Demonstrating how to sell is, of course, fraught with danger, or perhaps it is just embarrassment. Managers can have a bad day, too. But if the manager continually hides away from showing the trainee how to do it there is a danger of the salesperson believing that it cannot be done. Whatever happens, the fact that the manager has a go can earn undying loyalty, providing the same rules apply. A number of years ago I worked as a salesman for a major foods company and one week I had what I can only describe as an appalling week. In trepidation I returned to the office, where my manager blew a gasket. He took me out with him the next week determined to show me how it was done. On the first call he got the business, smirked till his face looked as though it would split in half, and said 'That's how it's done, son'. 'That's nice to know,' I replied. 'Does that mean I can now also offer 10 per cent more discount than I was allowed to last week?' We didn't get on too well after that, but at least he left me alone in future.

Consolidation of learning

At the end of the field visit both parties should reach an agreement on action for the next field visit. This may involve the manager agreeing to schedule a day out with the salesperson again very soon in order to improve a particular area. The salesperson may have to concentrate in the intervening period on some important area of improvement.

Whichever way you structure the content of your system, make sure that it remains flexible enough to cover any type of field training/coaching event. At the end of the visit both manager and salesperson should sign the field visit form shown in Figure 7.2, and this creates a contract. The contract for the manager is to help develop the knowledge and skills of the salesperson. The contract for the salesperson is to embark upon a self-development programme and to practise the skills covered on the field day.

The results of this and all other training events should be entered into a sales training recording system. An example is shown in Figure 7.3.

Professional sales training should be professionally recorded and form part of a total development and appraisal of skills. This is important information for trainers and can help you conduct a skills audit and check that training messages produced from the centre are being transmitted in the field. You should encourage trainers and managers to test for acceptance of the training message after each training event. For example, if a manager is covering the opening of a presentation on a field training day, does the trainee then learn that skill and use it? If the day has been about some area of knowledge improvement, what were the knowledge levels before and after? It is important to check these areas and to find a way to evaluate them in order to prove that training works. We will cover evaluation in a later chapter.

The last part of this system involves the keeping of a progress record. This is a motivational tool for both manager and salesperson. Everyone needs to know they are improving and managers need to know when they are being effective. You also need feedback on whether the training is working, the trainee is learning and improving, and the manager is developing into a good coach. Figure 7.4 shows the type of progress record you could use to monitor the improvement that trainees are making in the sales process. The letters under finding people, contacting people, and selling, refer to the subdivisions in Figure 6.5.

Sales Training Record			
Salesperson: **Start date:**			
Date	*Training event*	*Test*	*Comments*

Figure 7.3   Sales training recording system

Rules for field training events

There are some things that you need to train managers not to do, and others that you should encourage them to do:

- While most salespeople expect it, there should be no big lunches on field training days. It sometimes gets to the stage where that is all salespeople look forward to. It also shows that the manager is a provider of jelly beans and not of learning. Salespeople need to feel that they will benefit in terms of skills and knowledge development, not their waistlines. Taking trainees out to lunch sends a message to salespeople that management is about lunches, not about selling.
- There should never be any interruptions during a field training visit. Managers must never contact the office during the day. In my experience nothing happens during a day that cannot be left to the next day. It is highly likely that most managers have answering machines at home on which important messages can be left. The office should also be provided with an answering machine on which the manager can leave a reply and then someone in the office can take any appropriate action. The message to the salesperson when managers make telephone calls during field training says:

  You are not very important. What is really important is what is going on in the office. I, however, as a manager am very important, so much so that I cannot

Sales Process Progress Record								
Salesperson:			Start date:					
Evaluation date	Finding people			Contacting people			Selling		
	M	G	R	W	T	P	C	S	R

Key   1=Coaching needed   2=Little supervision   3=Train others

M=Market size   G=Geography   R=Resources
W=Writing   T=Telephoning   P=Personal calling
C=Communicating   S=Satisfying wants   R=Relationship
building

Figure 7.4   *Monitoring improvement in sales process*

leave the office for an hour in case something of vital importance comes up that I have to make decisions about.

- Teach managers not to gossip. It is bad enough for salespeople that managers at times appear to be the fount of all knowledge—they should not also appear to be the only person in the company to know what is going on. Managers should concentrate on the objective of the day, and not spread company and individual gossip. Managers are, however, very prone to doing this, as knowledge, and especially knowledge about other people, is power.

Sales meetings

Never allow a sales meeting to be conducted without a sales training session being included. Part of the overall training system that you introduce into the company should be a sales meeting training schedule of the type shown in Figure 7.5. I would suggest that the only purpose of a sales meeting is to carry out sales training. It is one of the few

Month	Date	Knowledge training	Skills training	Guest speakers	Duration
January					
February					
March					
April					
May					
June					
July					
August					
September					
October					
November					
December					

Figure 7.5   *Sales meeting training schedule*

times that a manager is able to communicate with the whole group an should be an event when those in the group who are succeeding can help those who are not.

There should be at least one sales meeting each month and sales trainers should be told in advance when and where they are to take place so that you can support these training events with either material or people. The schedule (Figure 7.5) is also a record of the continuous training that the company carries out and forms part of your evidence that the company delivers significantly more training days through your influence than simply those on a central programme.

Sales meetings also provide managers with an opportunity to motivate, a subject covered in more detail later.

Be wary, though, of managers who fill up their sales meetings with guest speakers instead of preparing a training session themselves. It is the manager's job to coach, not that of guest speakers. Every now and then introducing someone new helps, but it should be controlled. If you have to include a boring speaker, because they have some specialist knowledge, instead of letting them drone on for hours, have them interviewed by one of the salespeople. It is amazing how interesting even the most boring speaker can be when interviewed.

Key points

1 There is a saying—give a man a fish and you feed him for a day, but teach a man to fish and you feed him for a lifetime. A sales manager's job is about teaching others to do for themselves what managers cannot achieve on their own. The primary function of a sales manager is to coach.
2 The transfer of learning to the field is the responsibility of the sales manager, and must be done immediately after a central training event.
3 The involvement of managers in field training reinforces the messages given on the central sales training course.
4 Field training involves the four-part process of setting objectives, observing, giving feedback, and demonstration.
5 A field visit system which has the blessing and involvement of the MD will ensure that learning is being transferred from courses to the field.
6 As part of the overall development of the salesforce, training records should be introduced and monitored. The collection and maintenance of data is an important part of determining current and future training needs.
7 Sales meetings are opportunities for group sales training sessions and should not be used for items that could be dealt with in the post.

Recommended reading

Anderson, R.E., J.F. Hair and A.J. Bush, *Professional Sales Management*, McGraw-Hill 1988.

8 Motivation

This chapter aims to answer these questions:

- What is motivation in selling?
- How important is motivation in sales training?
- Whose responsibility is it to motivate salespeople?

The Oxford Illustrated Dictionary defines the word motivation as 'that which induces a person to act, e.g. desire, fear, circumstance'.

The topic of motivation is given great emphasis in the subjects of selling and sales management, and I do not intend to review that attention here other than to refer to its place in sales training and the shared responsibilities of trainer and manager.

It is a sales trainer's responsibility to motivate people to learn on courses and then the responsibility passes to the manager to transfer that learning into the field. Some say that it is not possible to motivate people but only to create an environment in which people can motivate themselves, and this is true up to a point. It does not mean, however, that trainers and managers can simply shrug their shoulders and abdicate all responsibility in the process.

Motivation to learn

We have already discussed the subject of attitude and the need to train your own salespeople in your own way. Acquisition of knowledge and the practice of skills is a matter of motivation. If salespeople are motivated to learn then they will. If they are motivated to change their behaviours then they will, but I do believe that sales trainers have a duty to make people learn. I also understand that this is not easy. Sales managers have said to me that you cannot motivate the unmotivated and I have had cases of people not wanting to listen and leaving courses having learned nothing. What you must do, however, is give it your best shot— put 'life' into your teaching and make it so interesting that trainees will want to learn.

Thomas Kopp talks about the problem of motivational factors in training and development and quotes Jane Marsh's research in 1983 where a trainee said:

I was so bored. An amazing burst of wishy-washiness had come over me, total lethargy, I'd got beyond caring, all stations closing down, you know. It was like compartments closing off when a ship is sinking, sort of getting down to the minimum space in your brain.

Kopp explains the prevalence of boredom on courses as being symptomatic of the way in which people have been conditioned to believe that classroom learning is supposed to be boring, compared with the instant gratification offered by the current entertainment media.

My own solution is that if you can't beat them you had better join them. It is important to make your training not just interesting but enjoyable. By this I don't mean it should be a laugh a minute, but it should make people feel good. It should convince trainees that there is something in the programme for them, that they are growing as human beings, and that the programme does not simply deal with work issues but includes material they can use in their own lives.

On the point about humour, I did say before that I do not like those training films that are saturated with humour, and I stand by that, but I think that humour has a place in training. Showing too many films with comedians in them merely reinforces the media entertainment message that learning is boring but leisure is always fun. Humour delivered live by the trainer can and does produce a totally different learning environment to that seen on film. Think about the last time you went to a live concert or a play—wasn't it ten times better than watching it on film?

Learning is the same. A good sales trainer, and there are too few around, can enliven the most dry content of a training course. It is the trainer who makes the material interesting and not vice versa. The material needs to be good in its content, I accept that, but a good sales trainer can use poor material and make it sound extremely important and very interesting. Kovach's research in 1987 showed quite clearly that what motivated employees more than any other item was interesting work. The same applies with sales training. The mistake is to believe that interesting sales training begins and ends with the material.

This is where organizations make their biggest and costliest mistake, by buying in someone else's material. The greatest mistake of all that they make is not to get that author to work with their sales managers and sales trainers and show them how to do it properly. The problem is that the last choice takes too long. In today's world a quick return on investment is desired, yet anything that is worth having requires pain and takes time.

Good sales trainers have the ability to show trainees that not only do they have a lot to learn but that everyone also has a great capacity for learning. Anyone who is interested in the power of the human brain and its capacity to absorb and use information, and the change and growth that is possible, should avail themselves of a Tony Buzan book or course. His coverage and knowledge of the subject of brain power is far greater than mine and his material is a joy to read.

What stops people from learning?

Much of our capacity for learning has come from the past and in particular early childhood. The way in which we were encouraged to ask questions and the manner in which the answers were given all played a part in formulating our attitudes towards learning. Accepting that the past got us where we are today, a great many people fail to realize that we are in control of the future. While our attitudes towards learning may be the result of the attitudes and skills instilled in us by trainers, our parents and teachers, our future acceptance and learning of new knowledge and skills rests with us as individuals. If you have yourself received any training in basic psychology or embarked upon any substantial reading on the subject you will understand what I mean. The problem with the vast majority of trainees going through training programmes is that they do not understand enough about themselves or their psychological history and so fail to activate the correct responses to learning opportunities.

Barriers to learning are deep-rooted. In some cases, it may be a lack of intelligence and therefore a failure to understand some of the concepts of selling that you intend to cover. There have been times when I have been faced with a lack of intelligence, often indicated by aggressive or non-assertive behaviour, and struggled to find a way to get through. For training to work, selection must work, and that is one of the reasons you must be involved in the selection process. For your sales training to work, you need good-quality raw material. Even the best of teachers cannot teach the unteachable.

Those without sales experience may have fixed attitudes about selling and salespeople. Just because someone is with your company as a salesperson does not mean they want to be in sales. No one leaves the educational system wanting to be a salesperson. Most people go into selling because their options start to close down in other occupations, or because they see the rewards in selling are potentially greater, or selling appears to bring with it a greater degree of freedom. Salespeople, telling others what they do, tend to omit the pain, failure and rejection from their job descriptions. People get into selling because they were sold the job.

It would not surprise me to learn that many people on your courses find the job, as explained by trainers, far removed from their preconceptions of the job when they applied. People at selection processes listen only to the benefits of the job and ignore the down-side. Managers interviewing candidates for sales roles concentrate on benefits and play down the negatives of selling. This presents you with problems over motivation to learn. Having realized they are in the wrong job even before they get out on the road, new salespeople are hardly likely to take in some of the difficult attitudinal changes you may be proposing on a sales training programme.

What can you do about it? In some ways it is too late to change the employment decision but you can restrict the damage either by discussing the situation with the trainee or talking to the trainee's manager.

One thing you should do, anyway, is to complete an evaluation of the trainee, a subject discussed in the next chapter.

Your biggest problems could be with those who already have sales experience. People with sales experience have built up emotional walls which they use to protect themselves from rejection. While acknowledging it externally, any criticism of them or their style of selling rarely gets through. It is a self-preserving mechanism that makes the acceptance of new ideas a rare occurence. Experienced salespeople are usually only interested in how to overcome objections and learning a new closing technique. So how do you get through to them? Only a good sales trainer can, and even then it takes time and the failure rate is substantial. It highlights the need for managers to take over salespeople immediately after the central programme and reinforce the message already covered.

Change takes time and is painful, especially for those already in selling. Salespeople trying out new behaviours will look and sound uncomfortable at first. It is your job and that of the manager to help trainees through this difficult learning curve. The influence of the manager here is crucial. You know that learning new behaviours takes time but time is precious in selling and for new starters there is always the pressure of targets. 'Do I just get on with it and sell as best I know how, or do I learn this new skill and risk failure?' The answer is usually the former and, subsequently, peak performance is rare. New salespeople regard those who are successful as the ideal, and attempt to change to their styles overnight. It is doubtful whether you could emulate someone else, anyway, but overnight successes are uncommon.

Finding it too difficult to change into successful salespeople, there is a tendency to use unsuccessful salespeople as role models. Listening to other salespeople's failures and problems is comforting, especially if their complaints are to do with company policies and impossible targets. Be wary of exposing your trainees too early to those in the company who are not achieving. The learning process is difficult enough without the message coming from those who are failing that the theoretical training does not work in practice.

There is a game I know called 'Neg Jamborees', an event at which negative people gather. It takes place at sales conferences and there are subcommittees at sales meetings, and branches exist wherever salespeople meet. This is where the real selling is done. Unsuccessful salespeople sell their failure to those close to success but not quite achieving it. They have been around since time began. They are convinced of a world that was flat; that man couldn't fly; and that success in selling relies upon either cheating or luck. Where 'Neg Jamborees' are happening it is raining all the time. In some cases there are torrential downpours. As a sales trainer you have to begin with selling umbrellas and progress to taking people where the sun shines. I don't mean that you can ignore the rain—if it rains it rains—but you have a choice—to stay where it is raining, or to go where you can guarantee more sunshine than rain. Sales trainers have a duty to get salespeople to under-stand that the choice is theirs. It is not destined that they be failures, no more than it is destined that they be successful. What is guaranteed is that the destiny of success lies within each individual. To be more suc-cessful than in the past, however, something has to change—either the internal or the external environment. If it is external factors, then they will have to wait for luck. If it is internal, then you can help them.

Confidence in the trainer

Trainees will want to learn if they believe the trainers know what they are talking about and if they hold a position of authority in the company. Sales trainers must be competent. They must know about psychology, communication, learning, training technique, and they must be able to sell.

It is important that trainees can empathize with the trainer and vice versa, so trainers need to be able to show that they have sold and understand the problems associated with the sales job. Credibility in selling is very important and no more so than credibility in the sales trainer. The trainer must be able to talk about the job and how to do it without constantly referring to training notes. If trainers use a highly structured approach to the training event it makes trainees feel insecure about the trainer's capability. If trainers rely on experience it makes their audience feel that they know what they are talking about. It is very difficult to talk without notes if you have no first-hand experience.

Trainers must have status in the company. Salespeople only listen to those with power. If, in your training role, you have no power then all you will get from salespeople is problems. Without power and status you will be no more than a stoker on a ship—you fuel the engines but the boys in the uniforms on the bridge decide the ship and the ship's company's fate. As a trainer without power you may have influence out-side the training arena, but selling, whether women are in the team or not, is a 'macho' business, and acceptance of messages begins with the premise: 'Who is that person? Why should I listen to them?' The only people salespeople listen to are managers and those in authority. That is why trainers need authority and that is why managers have to be given the responsibility for further training and development of their teams.

The intervention of the trainer as a catalyst in the learning event cannot be over-emphasized.

Motivation to learn will be stimulated by sessions that centre on teaching trainees about themselves. The activity may not always be comfortable, but it is compulsive. Most people, saints apart, are self-centred. Most people ask themselves 'What's in it for me?' Whether relevant to the training or not, always try to include some form of questionnaire or review or video training in which trainees feel they have learned some-thing about themselves. If you tell people at the beginning of a training programme that you will be providing them with an insight into their sales personality, or will give them a report on their progress at the end of the course, or a video showing themselves, it will stimulate both enthusiasm and attention.

Motivation to learn is paramount. You can only teach people so much. For me the job of a sales trainer is as much about stimulating people to want to learn more, as training them to do the current job.

Self-motivation

Is is possible to give people self-motivation? I believe it is, although there are few people who can do it. It depends on whether your company recognizes the importance of sales training and understands that the country has very few excellent sales trainers. By 'excellent' I mean those few sales trainers who can motivate salespeople to want to sell, to want to learn, and to want to succeed. It may sound strange to say that salespeople have to be motivated to want to succeed, but my experience shows that salespeople devote more energy to a fear of failure than to a desire to succeed.

Success in selling is a mixture of external and internal factors. The external factors come with the job and include knowledge, experience and—more than anything else—the influence of the sales manager. Internal factors are those things that come from inside—self-motivation and the right attitude. You cannot guarantee that trainees will arrive with evidence of either on the surface, and it is the job of the sales trainer to get trainees to dig deep within themselves and find the motivation that should be there. It is said that you cannot train people how to sell, they have to want to. I would also say that it is the sales trainer's job to sell salespeople the want.

We have already said that people buy what they want, not what they need, and salespeople are no different. They will buy what your training programme has to offer if you can prove to them that they really want it. The answer is easy but at the same time difficult. If they do not want to change they will stay exactly where they are now. You will hear a lot of nonsense about how successful they have been already, but the chances are high that they will have joined you because they have failed to realize their ambitions elsewhere.

An open mind

I usually begin each sales training course with a talk on the importance of keeping an open mind. Unless you tackle this problem at the beginning of a sales training event you run the risk of trying to train zombies. Many salespeople attend courses not because they want to be there but because they have been told to be there. That does nothing for the learning possibilities, and even less for your self-confidence. Sales trainers should begin training events with a couple of rules. Mine are simple.

The first is keeping an open mind. Like reading this book—you can adopt the attitude that you've read it all before, and there is nothing new in it. Similarly, there will be a number of people who attend your courses and say they have heard it all before. Both premises are impossible. The significance of keeping an open mind was poignantly brought home to me a number of years ago. My son was about nine years old at the time, and had taken up an interest in fishing. Because of his age I used to accompany him. I felt uncomfortable leaving him on his own, and in any case there are few enough moments for a father and son to spend time together. As he got older, I took less part. I still went, but I spent more and more time in the car, writing, reading, and thinking about writing this book.

It was rare, especially in the early days, to catch anything at all, and yet his enthusiasm was never dampened. However, when he did catch a fish, the excitement was unbridled. I also could not empathize with why Michael was keen to return to the same spot, sometimes day after day, whether he caught anything or not. We used to sit for hours without a bite and, while I would wander up and down the canal looking for a more productive pitch, he would sit and wait. He also kept a log in which he wrote the time of day; the water conditions; the weather; the type of bait used; the line; the float; and a whole list of other information. Then I understood. He knew a lot more about life and the changing nature of life than ever I had done. While I saw the same place at the canal bank; the same water; conditions; and it has to be said the most appalling bait, the reality was quite different. Each micro second that passed produced a change. The water that passed was always changing. The fish moved and were replaced. The weather was never the same, and naturally enough even though we used the same type of bait, it was obviously never the same bait. His enthusiasm for fishing came from an approach that every fishing event was new.

I felt ashamed of the time I had wasted, and in reviewing how I had spent certain periods of my life was overwhelmed by a sense of having been cheated by time. How many people attend your courses or indeed drift through life believing that they have been there before, seen it all before, and know it all. What I say is 'You might have heard it before—but you have never heard it from me. You might have even heard it from me, but you've never heard it from me today'.

Life is too short to be doing things that waste it. Unfortunately, a great many people create their own wasted life through the attitude they adopt to learning and growth. I insist that unless people approach my training events with a totally open mind that says 'Forget what you know—this is new', then they would be better off doing something else. Don't let people waste their time and, more importantly, yours by closing their minds to what could be the most important training event of their lives.

Remaining positive

My second rule is about being positive. It is imperative that your trainees grasp the importance of approaching the learning task in a positive frame of mind. Your problem is that you will be faced with more failing salespeople than successful ones, and that in itself will expose you and them to negative attitudes. Negativity is a cancer which spreads throughout all sales teams and has to be tackled head on. Your duty is to expose it on sales courses, shaming people whose negativity is stopping them from being as successful as they have the potential to be. You and they need to spend time, especially at the beginning of a sales training event, examining the motivational factors affecting salespeople.

What motivates salespeople is debatable. Kovach, in 1987, produced a paper that examined the results of previous research into employee motivation. The factors swung from recognition as the main motivator to interesting work. I favour the work carried out by Shipley and Keily in the early 1980s which shows that salespeople are motivated by reward, recognition and achievement.

It could be seen as somewhat glib to say that your learning events should be rewarding, that people should be recognized for having learned new skills and that they should gain a sense of achievement from your training programme, and yet this is exactly what you have to do.

The reward from your training programme is that salespeople will achieve more as a result of following your suggestions. That means that you should carry out a full and researched evaluation of the effect of your training, as explained in the next chapter. People who are seen to try out new skills on your programme should receive recognition. You should award prizes for the best presentations even if it is just a certificate. It is important that managers understand the importance of reward and recognition when training salespeople in the field. It is from these rewards and recognition that salespeople get a sense of achievement. Research in the 1950s showed that the highest level of human motivation comes from a sense of achievement and recent research reinforces these theories. Modern salespeople have different values from their 1950s counterparts, and achievement is derived from reward and recognition. The three are inexorably linked.

Winner and Schiff's research in 1980 found that salespeople placed a high priority on financial reward as a main motivating factor in job performance. Making more money was specified as an important motivator. Your training programme must be seen as a way of meeting these demands.

If reward is the primary motivating factor for salespeople, then you must link your training events with that by getting trainees to establish early on in the training event what it is they want from the sales job. Your training should be seen as a method of obtaining just that. There is a price, however—they appreciate that nothing in life is free. The price, though, may be worth the benefit they derive. Staying positive is part of the price. It is far more comfortable to succumb to negative attitudes than positive, and peer pressure on negativity is common-place. We would all be extremely upset and probably annoyed with anyone who emptied a dustbin of rubbish onto our living room carpet. Why is it then that we seem not to object to people regularly dumping rubbish on our minds? Negative attitudes are far worse than the rubbish in a bin, and your mind is infinitely more expensive to replace than your carpet.

The point of all this is that the sales trainers have a responsibility to motivate people to want to learn, but, to do that, everyone needs to understand fully the problems faced from closed minds and negative attitudes. Somewhere along the line, you as a trainer have to create your own stories and analogies, and they don't come out of books or exist in other people's training notes. They come from experience, and especially experience of having been there yourself. Good sales trainers have a history of success and of failure, and they recognize the pressures of selling.

Pressure

To understand fully how salespeople learn, all those involved in training them need also to be aware of the pressures of the job. Pressure in selling is a two-edged sword (see Figure 8.1). On the one hand there are the emotional pressures of self-motivation and the ever-present feeling of rejection. On the other there are the physical pressures associated with selling. Selling is a physically draining activity. In many industries the salesperson is expected to know more than the managing director. As far as the customer is concerned, the salesperson *is* the company and the source of all knowledge. It is also the salesperson who receives all complaints.

The salesperson has to cope with internal and external rules, targets that begin again every year, competition, poor managers, and an ever-changing product range.

Managers and trainers need to be constantly aware of the pressures affecting the modern salesperson and how best to support this most

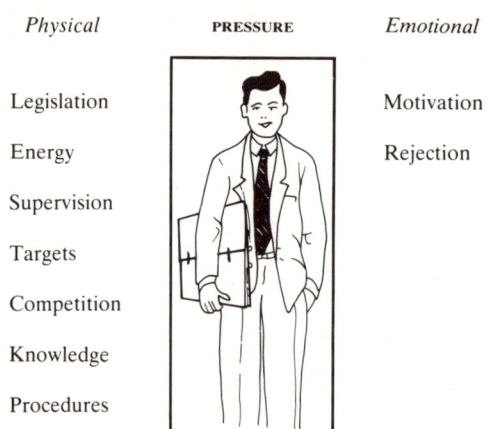

Physical	**PRESSURE**	*Emotional*
Legislation		Motivation
Energy		Rejection
Supervision		
Targets		
Competition		
Knowledge		
Procedures		

Figure 8.1   The pressures of selling

important person. There is no one motivational factor that works in all cases. Managers and trainers must have a broad knowledge of the subject of motivation so that they can adapt to each unique situation when it arises.

Part of that support is the training you give to salespeople. Even though the major request will most certainly be for product training, you know that attitude change is far likelier to result in performance change than additional product knowledge. I recognize that changing people's attitudes is not easy, and that the main drive for change will come from the individual salespeople themselves. So how can you influence that change?

In the first place you can influence change by the manner in which you deliver your central programme. I do believe that you can motivate people, but I also recognize that it can be short-lived. The trick, therefore, is to extend that motivation out into the field.

Second, maintaining enthusiasm happens through managers, and it is your job to prepare managers for the role they have in keeping that positive motivation going. But managers also need motivating, and part of your programme should contain motivational elements for sales managers. Their acceptance of the attitudinal training content of your programme will be far less than that of salespeople, though. Sales managers are considerably more insecure than salespeople, but better at hiding it. Many sales managers cannot believe their good fortune at getting out of front-line selling activity. Nevertheless, they are as susceptible as the next person to examining their own motivational factors, and can be made to feel ashamed when faced with a realization that they could have wasted long periods of their lives.

Self-training

Notwithstanding all this, motivation, and the creation of a motivational climate, does need constant refuelling. Some companies seek to achieve this with centrally run refresher courses, but I see this as the least effective way of recharging motivation. Next up the hierarchy is the practice of using sales managers, and I endorse this whole-heartedly. The most effective method, and probably the least used by companies and especially individuals, is self-training.

Some companies achieve this by distance-learning methods such as computer-based training, study manuals, or even interactive video. These methods are certainly useful for training salespeople not based in a central location and are primarily used for knowledge acquisition. Interactive video can be used for skills acquisition but is expensive, both in its original despatch and in updating, and beyond the reach of most training departments. It is also disputable whether selling skills can be learned through any other method except observation, coaching and practice.

So how can you apply distance-learning methods to motivation or attitude training? It is possible to create an open learning centre and I would favour this approach. Whether you call it that, or a resource centre, or simply a library is up to you, but the effect is the same for those who want to take part. The greatest problem is getting people to use it, especially a fragmented salesforce, but it is worth the effort. Sales jobs are lonely, and salespeople feel that sometimes the company fails to understand what it is like to be out doing the job while that lot at head office reap all the benefits of their labours. In setting up a resource centre which contains sales cassettes, videos, books and self-training material, you will be displaying a real concern for their continued personal self-development.

The availability of material in all these media is substantial, and I recommend that you allocate a proportion of your training materials budget to the provision of a source library for those salespeople interested in developing themselves. The chances are that, even though they may represent a small percentage of the total salesforce, they will most probably be the best performers. Getting an extra 5 per cent return from top performers can add significantly more to your bottom line than improving a poor performer by 25 per cent.

Key points

1 Motivation continues to be a hotly disputed subject, and what motivates salespeople in particular seems as elusive as ever.
2 The main motivator to learning is the sales trainer and it therefore follows that the main motivator to learning in the field is the sales manager.
3 Barriers to learning are deep-rooted and have more to do with past experiences than inability to learn.
4 It can be more difficult to change the skills of those with previous sales experience than to teach those without experience how to sell.
5 For trainees to be motivated to learn, and in some cases change, they must have confidence in the sales trainer. This will only be achieved if the sales trainer has had a successful track record in selling.
6 Sales trainers have a responsibility for creating the best learning environment by helping trainees examine their own open-mindedness and positive attitudes.
7 Distance learning methods can be used to provide salespeople with the opportunity for personal development through the provision of source material on selling, attitude development and self-motivation.

Recommended reading

Bettger, F. *How I raised myself from Failure to Success in Selling*, Cedar 1951.
Braysich, J. *The Complete Executive*, Joseph Braysich Australia 1986.
Buzan, T. *Use your Head*, BBC Books 1982.
Carnegie, D. *How to stop Worrying and start Living*, Cedar 1953.
Dowling W.F. and L.R. Sales. *How Managers Motivate: the imperatives of supervision*, McGraw-Hill 1971.
Hill, N. *Think and Grow Rich*, Wilshire Book Co. 1937.
Kreigel, R. *The C Zone: peak performance under pressure*, Cedar 1987.

Kushel, G. *The 4%*, Sigdwick & Jackson 1984.

Lakien, A. *How to get Control of your Time and your Life*, Gower 1984.

Mulligan, J. *The Personal Management Handbook: How to make the most of your potential*, Sphere 1988.

Peale, N.V. *The Power of Positive Thinking*, Cedar 1953.

Schwartz, D. *The Magic of Thinking Big*, Prentice Hall 1959.

Shipley D. and J. Keily. 'Motivation and dissatisfaction of industrial salespeople. How relevant is Hertzberg's theory?' *European Journal of Marketing* 22.1.1986.

Smiles, S. *Self-Help*, Penguin 1986.

Steers R.M. and L.W. Porter. *Motivation and Work Behaviour*, McGraw-Hill 1987.

Stern, and R. Zemke. *Stressless Selling*, Amacom 1990.

Tack, A. *Sell better, Live Better*, Cedar 1958.

Vroom, V.H. (Foreword) *Manage People, not Personnel*. Harvard Business 1990.

Zig Ziglar with Jim Savage. *Top Performance: How to develop excellence in yourself and others*, Fleming H. Revell Company 1986.

References

Kopp, T. 'Making trainees want to learn', *Training and Development Journal* June 1988.

Kovach, K. 'What motivates employees? Workers and supervisors give different answers'. *Business Horizons* Sep/Oct. 1987.

Shipley, D. and J. Keily. 'Industrial salesforce motivation and Herzberg's dual factor theory: a UK perspective', *Journal of Personal Selling and Sales Management* Vol. 6, no. 1. 1986.

Winner L. and J. Schiff. 'Industrial salespeople's views on motivation', *Industrial Marketing Management* Vol. 9. 1980.

9 Does it work?

This chapter aims to answer the following questions:

- What methods are used to evaluate sales training?
- Is it really possible to evaluate sales training or must it be looked at purely as an investment for the future?
- Who should evaluate sales training?

Evaluation

Evaluation has been described by Hamblin as 'any attempt to obtain information on the effects of a training programme, and to assess the value of the training in the light of that information'. If this is true, and I go along with this definition, most sales trainers that I am aware of miss out altogether by evaluating only at an immediate reaction level, if at all. Even Hamblin has said that evaluation of sales training is as difficult as trying to evaluate management training and this has given many trainers the excuse for not trying to ascertain the cost benefits of sales training.

For many trainers the criteria against which to evaluate are too difficult to establish. Evaluation is complicated by many variables—geography, demography, marketing conditions, experience, managers, attitudes, timing—and product launches only scratch the surface of the obstacles in the way of getting to grips with measuring sales training effectiveness. Honeycutt and Stevenson also found that most companies carried out only immediate reaction evaluation at the most, and a significant number conducted no evaluations at all.

Cummings has said that the objective of sales training is that after a training event salespeople should observe an increase in performance, and I feel this is a reasonable assumption. The proviso is that the sales trainer is able to influence what happens after the training event. When Snader says that sales training doesn't work he qualifies it by saying that the reasons are to do with poor sales management follow-up. He used an athletic analogy saying that it would be unheard of for an athlete after training not to continually receive further coaching.

O'Neill also says that there is a continuing need for managers to be more involved in training salespeople. The reason? As Robinson so clearly puts it: 'How a trainee performs on a course is no indication whatsoever as to how he will perform in the job, and the latter is the ultimate measure of the usefulness of the training'.

The greatest problem faced by sales trainers is that the assumption is made that what is practised on a central course is also practised in the field. This is a dangerous assumption and many sales courses have floundered because of inadequate sales management follow-up. This situation focuses attention on the question of whether to evaluate the course itself or its outcome. Which you choose has more to to with the influence you have on follow-up. Unless you have direct influence on the quantity, quality and timing of field coaching, then you can only evaluate the training event. If you have control of the post-course mechanisms then you can evaluate the effect of the training.

In some cases salespeople have also been sent on sales training courses merely as a precursor to being dismissed, after all else had failed to motivate the individual to peak performance. 'Send him on a course with Joe . . . that will put him right.' It would obviously be very difficult to evaluate whether sales training had been successful in such a case, but then perhaps that is half the problem.

End-of-course evaluations

On one level evaluation of sales training, or any training for that matter, appears to be a simple process. The most common application of evaluation happens in the form of post-course evaluation by trainees. It is rare to find any evaluation procedures that involve line managers, either evaluating their follow-up of sales training or seeking any evaluation from them of the effectiveness of the training delivered. In my experience most forms of evaluation are pointless and evaluate very little.

Trainers over the country seem to collect volumes of meaningless data which in most cases merely stroke their egos. My own research showed that the nearer to a training event the end-of-course evaluation was, the more favourable the evaluation turned out to be.

If you do want a measure of objectivity from trainees about the worth of a course, you should not have them complete an end-of-course evaluation, but send out an evaluation questionnaire at least six weeks after the event. This allows trainees to get over the euphoria of the training event and analyse whether the content of the course has any practical relevance. Even then there is a problem. What happens if trainees have not tried out your methods in the field? Does that mean that your methods do not work? What happens if trainees have tried your methods only once or twice, found them uncomfortable, and gone back to old habits or developed some poor ones of their own? Is that a fair evaluation of the training? What about the situation in which the line manager disagrees with your training methods, for whatever reason? Does that mean that your training does not work?

In current practices the true evaluation of sales training seems to be as remote as ever. Asking trainees to evaluate sales training courses has a worth equal only to what each individual trainee personally gets out of a course. Even then, how do you evaluate a course if you did not want to be there?

I see no value in end-of-course evaluations. If you do want a measure of what is going on after the training event, an evaluation form sent out two or three months afterwards, along the lines of that shown in Appendix 1, seems of more use. You may have to accept that the longer you leave trainee evaluations, the less response you will get. Within three months, you could get as little as 20 per cent response.

The benefits, however, could be that you collect some interesting data from the responses which could help you formulate and refine some of your training policies. My own research, using this type of question-naire, revealed the following data:

- 93 per cent of salespeople I surveyed (n.135) said they believed that customers buy from people they like. I found this contradicted the impression that trust and likability factors were thought less important then sales skills (100 per cent).
- While 71 per cent of salespeople agreed that practising selling skills regularly was important, 43 per cent also felt that role play was irrel-evant. I have observed that many salespeople have a great reluctance to role play. In most professions practice plays a large part in devel-oping skills and is the key to excellence in performance. In selling, however, salespeople steadfastly refuse to want to be involved in practising their skill. This resistance to role play may also account for the high failure rate among salespeople. It seems that salespeople get their practice in real sales situations. Salespeople, in order to be suc-cessful, require a high self-image. It would appear that displaying inadequacies in front of their colleagues is either embarrassing or an indication of weakness. Whatever the reason, it is a measure of how useless it is to ask salespeople for an objective evaluation of courses. They are unlikely to rate highly any course that concentrates too much on role play, and yet as a professional trainer I know that it is role play that determines how effectively trainees learn a new skill. (The only reason that sales courses are not completely occupied with role play is that it is boring and tiring for trainers.)
- 21 per cent felt there was no such thing as the 'natural born sales wonder'. But a massive 86 per cent also believed that, even given the same training, most people could not be as good at selling as they were themselves. What they were really saying was that there are no natural born sales wonders apart from themselves. My experience has consistently shown that experienced salespeople, and especially sales managers, have the impression that everyone needs training apart from them.
- Many of the findings were contradictory, highlighting, perhaps, the insecurity of many salespeople. When I put a similar question about the need for training in a different format I was told by 80 per cent that sales training was imperative. The same 80 per cent also felt that the trainer's influence was of greater importance than the content of the training. Once again, however, arrogance prevailed when nearly 40 per cent said they could have survived without any sales training

at all. I also found that there was a remarkable amount of loyalty shown by trainees to the trainer, whether trainees succeeded in the job or not. Having received training from a motivational trainer, salespeople seem loathe to level any criticism at the trainer, or the content, given that both were initially accepted. Salespeople not accepting either the trainer or content on first encounter blamed both for subsequent failure but did not change their views if initially the reaction was positive.

- With regard to attitude training, 70 per cent felt that the motivational content of the course helped them to cope with the stresses and pressures of the job, with at least 50 per cent also believing that they had changed in terms of their own attitudes. Thirty per cent even said that others had noticed significant positive changes in their attitude after the sales course. Disappointingly, a consistent 50 per cent of salespeople I canvassed reported that they received little or no motivation from their line managers. It would seem that salespeople see the importance of a positive attitude in selling as do many sales managers. Most evaluations fail to ask questions about attitude building.
- Having got into selling (99 per cent did not choose it as their first career), 70 per cent felt that they would always be in selling. A group of 35 per cent, however, had strong management aspirations. This confirms my previous research which shows that many salespeople see sales management as a way of getting out of selling. Every time, those with that attitude also failed in sales management.
- Does sales training work? Ninety per cent thought it did.

Pre-course expectations

Some time ago there was a vogue to elicit material from trainees about their expectations of a proposed course. In this way courses could be tailored to suit the needs of a particular group. My research in this area showed that trainees have little to add to the structuring of sales training courses. If you are interested in confirming my own findings, you could issue a pre-course questionnaire along the lines of that in Appendix 2.

My research concentrated on a group of experienced trainees who were asked to determine what percentage of time should be spent on a sales course in a particular area. Their answers were:

	%
• Product knowledge	18
• Attitude and self-awareness	17
• Selling theory	15
• Role play	12
• Buyer behaviour	12
• Group discussions	10
• Company policy and aims	8

I fed this information about the average group perceptions of how to allocate training time back to the group and then asked them to change any percentages if they wished (Appendix 3). None did.

The actual time allocations I had made in this particular series of courses was as follows:

	%
• Product knowledge	27
• Attitude and self-awareness	9
• Selling theory	25
• Role play	21
• Buyer behaviour	4
• Group discussions	9
• Company policy and aims	5

Faced with discrepancies, what do you do? Who is right and who is wrong? It seems as pointless asking trainees what they want to learn, in what time slots, as it is asking school children what they would like to see on the curriculum. If trainers are the professionals, then they should decide what is to be learned, how it is to be taught, and what time is to be spent on it.

Another difficulty with evaluation is that sales training, like management training, has much to do with change of behaviour and that is something that can never be achieved overnight. It would be naive for any manager to believe that by sending someone on a sales training course they will return sufficiently motivated to increase their performance immediately, when the answer to improved performance probably lies much closer to home.

I believe that the true evaluation of sales training can only be achieved if the following elements exist:

1 Behaviour of trainees is monitored before the training event.
2 Behaviour is discussed with the trainee, and agreement is reached as to the nature and pattern of that behaviour.
3 It is recognized by everyone concerned (trainee, trainer, manager) that no one behavioural style is correct.
4 Behaviour during the training event is monitored, and compared with initial behaviour; the trainee is involved in the process of comparison.
5 Trainees are taught to recognize varying behavioural styles, and how to alter their own style in order to communicate effectively with others.
6 Immediately after the training event, behaviour is monitored in the field and finely tuned.
7 Training is continuous.

Even if it was common practice to evaluate the outcome of training, it would be difficult to determine whether increased performance occurred as a result of training, management intervention, or both. So where do you begin?

Accountability

A good place to start would be in deciding who is accountable for the outcome of sales training. It is obvious that it cannot be the trainer unless the trainer and the line manager are the same person. For anyone to want something to succeed they need ownership. Trainers who are not line managers cannot therefore have ownership of the long-term success of sales training without some kind of authority to ensure that behaviour in the field with regard to the trainee matches the behaviour taught on the course. Within this premise lies the crux of the problem. Most organizations will not give trainers the authority to insist that certain managerial actions are carried out in the field post-course. Without this authority trainers cannot be held accountable for the outcome of training if the desired outcome is sales success.

Without this agreement there will always exist the 'them and us' syndrome. For sales training to be evaluated on a basis of whether it works in the field or not, you must decide what sales trainers are accountable for, what managers are accountable for, and allocate authority accordingly.

If sales trainers are only accountable for changes in trainee behaviour while trainees are under the influence of the trainer, then the system proposed earlier will work well enough. That is not to say that it is not difficult, especially with regard to resources, but it is possible. Before this, however, there has to be total agreement between managers and trainers about the ideal behaviours being taught.

Sales managers It is clear to me that managers are responsible for the performance of their salespeople. It is the manager who has the greatest influence on the individual salesperson following a training event, and it should therefore be the manager who is accountable for sales training after the central foundation training. This means that it is managers' training of trainees that should be evaluated.

The whole point of sales training is that it should add value to the company's results. It would therefore be naive of sales trainers to assume that they alone can ensure an increase in sales performance through centralized sales training without the assistance and follow-up of the sales manager.

The point about sales training is whether the money spent on training has been an investment or a cost. If an investment, then a return is required. This means that you have to create the environment in which you can prove that there is a competitive advantage to be gained from structuring your training in such a way that you can not only justify the expenditure but also demand more.

Training experienced salespeople— the effects It is easier to determine the effect of training on experienced salespeople than that on new starters. With experienced salespeople you simply include the following procedures:

1 Record the results of the group attending the course for a time period of not less than eight weeks before the training event.

2 Set up a control group within the same areas that the salespeople work in.
3 Take an average of the performances of other areas.
4 Run the training event.
5 Carry out the same analyses for eight weeks after the training event.
6 Calculate exactly how much it cost for the salespeople to attend the training event. To do this you must include the following costs:
  • total cost of the trainers (inclusive of benefits) (T)
  • development and materials costs (D)—it would be usual for one day's training to take ten days to develop
  • venue and travelling costs (V)
  • the lost sales opportunity of the salespeople attending the event (S)
7 Calculate the yearly benefit of the results:
  • increase in sales per year of the group as compared to sales prior to the training event (I)
8 Subtract the cost from the benefit, and you will be able to calculate the return on investment (ROI).
9 Compare these results to the control groups.

Example

Suppose that a training event is scheduled for one day and has ten trainees:

T = £20 000 + £12 000 (benefits) / 225 (average working days) = £142.00. (Be sure to take into account the number of trainers attending.)

D = £1420 + £500 (materials) = £1920.

V = £1500 (Total cost of the venue, including travelling costs, for the duration of the event, whether in total delegates rates or complete costing for own premises.)

S = £500 × 10 trainees = £5000

$T+D+V+S$ = £8562.00

I = 225 (available working days) × £100 = £22 500

$ROI = I - (T+D+V+S)$

£22 500 − £8562 = £13 938

= 54%

Getting returns on investment of this kind are not unusual. Having carried out this analysis a number of times, I have recorded returns in excess of 400% in the past. There is also a further hidden benefit, in that the development charge, while absorbed on one training event, has cost benefits for future training events. The next time the event is scheduled there is little development work to do.

Another way to prove that your training is a high-return and low-risk investment is to have all trainees attending a course complete a pledge (Figure 9.1) that they will generate an extra amount of business in return for the training delivered. Line managers can then also use this pledge to monitor post-training performance and correct it when it goes

Contract

This contract exists between . . . . and the training department.

In return for a training course which will help you to develop the skills necessary to carry out your sales role, the department has invested in you a sum of £ . . . .

The company sees this as an investment in your training and personal development which will within . . . . months realize a return of £ . . . .

Signed . . . .
(training department)

Signed . . . .
(trainee)

Figure 9.1 *Sample contract between trainee and training department*

adrift from the agreed objectives. This signing of a pledge also seals the contract between the trainer and the line manager.

These are relatively simple methods of proving how effective your training is. The important thing is to make certain that you carry out some form of evaluation which is results-oriented. Without this, you and your department will always be at a disadvantage when it comes to budgetary cut-backs. Other methods are also discussed at length in Jack Phillips's excellent book on evaluation listed at the end of this chapter.

Training new starters—the effect

The most difficult thing to ascertain is whether or not your training has any significant influence on the performance of people joining the company. This difficulty is rarely faced, and so most companies are totally unaware of whether their induction training is of any use. It also presents further problems: unless you are able to evaluate these initial courses, how do you know how much time to spend on any particular topic? As mentioned earlier, discrepancies exist between what trainees say they want and what trainers say works. And, as with all experts, between trainers it is also impossible to reach agreement. So how long should you spend on any particular element?

What you need is data, and the only way to get data is to:

1 Monitor average results of trainee groups using one method of training and compare with average results of other salespeople in the field.
2 Calculate the trends and compare.
3 Change your training and do the same calculations.

In the first instance, what do you do if the trend for new starters is less than existing staff? Does this mean that your training is having a detrimental effect? It may not be so, but the question is worth asking. Having asked the question and shared it with operational management, you will gain significantly more credibility than if you fail to carry out any such evaluations.

At some stage you and the line managers will have to take the bull by the horns and find out what happens to people who receive no initial sales training. Only by doing this will you find out whether your company's foundation sales training works or not. My research shows that those who receive no induction sales training fare worse than those who do. Only you can determine whether the results for your own training are similar.

Evaluating the trainer

The usual type of evaluation carried out on trainers resembles that shown in Figure 9.2 and in essence there is not a lot wrong with it. You can design your own depending on what you want to know. Do you want to know how the trainer is perceived by the trainees or do you want to know if the trainer is doing a professional job?

In one sense, providing the trainer has some influence on post-course activity, whether directly or via a field training system run by managers, it should be easy to monitor results as a way of calculating if the trainer is effective or not. Without a guaranteed follow-up by managers, however, it would be unreasonable to expect the trainer to influence performance for more than two weeks after the event. My research shows that the effects of a first-class sales trainer can be expected to last only for a maximum of 21 days following a training event. That said, a line manager can destroy a whole training programme in less than 24 hours.

If you don't have a follow-up agreement with line managers of the sort I have already outlined, then the best you can do is hope to balance your books on a ten-day improvement in performance. The only way to do this is to run non-residential workshops for large numbers of salespeople and hope for some divine intervention. If your company continues to expect this sort of performance from you, I suggest you find a better

---

Trainer's Evaluation

Name of trainer . . . .

Expresses ideas clearly	1	2	3	4	5	6	7	Confusing
Made sessions interesting	1	2	3	4	5	6	7	Boring
Time poorly organized	7	6	5	4	3	2	1	Time well organized
Examples used were clear and relevant	1	2	3	4	5	6	7	Poor use of examples
Presentation style enjoyable	1	2	3	4	5	6	7	I did not enjoy presentation style
Voice modulation poor	7	6	5	4	3	2	1	Voice modulation good
Related well to me	1	2	3	4	5	6	7	Showed little empathy
Sincere	1	2	3	4	5	6	7	Insincere

Figure 9.2 *Format for trainer evaluation*

company to work for. Sales training is stressful enough without having to aim for the impossible.

The only person qualified to evaluate the trainer is another trainer. Only another sales trainer can give a fair appraisal of the performance of a peer. The format can be similar to that in Figure 9.2 but oral feedback and discussion should also be allowed for. Trainers do not like criticism, no matter how constructive. Some years ago I used a system where trainees evaluated sales trainers, without oral feedback and discussion. The results were startling in terms of the animosity created among the trainers, with accusations of falsified results and irrelevant data. Feeding back training performance to a trainer is a sensitive issue and should be handled by a professional.

Evaluating trainees

It is also important for trainers to give managers feedback on the performance of trainees, whether they be existing staff or new starters. My research showed that trainers were 50 per cent more likely to spot failures than were managers on selection processes. Obviously, trainers have more time to monitor new starters than managers can spend on recruitment interviews, but the results suggest that managers need to spend a lot longer looking at applicants before employing them. Many companies use a system of pre-contract training, which I would recommend. It can be expensive to offer training to people who do not work for you but want to, but the long-term benefits of making more objective selection decisions far outweigh the initial cost. It also sorts out those who are not really committed in the first place.

Appendix 4 shows the sort of evaluation format you could use to evaluate trainees. The greatest problem will be collecting objective data. It is relatively easy to feed back to managers the results of knowledge acquisition. When it comes to skills or attitude, you must be careful about the subjective nature of your comments. In any event, feedback to managers has to be confidential, and should only be used by the manager as a means of confirming positive or negative results in the field. The worst possible thing a manager can do on the return of a trainee from a course is to say, 'Well, it seems that the trainer thinks you're a totally useless article. Have you anything to say about that?'

But then your managers wouldn't do that, would they?

Key points

1 Evaluating sales training programmes is as difficult as evaluating the worth of management training programmes.
2 A large number of companies find the process of evaluating sales training so difficult that they do not bother.
3 Immediate reaction evaluations are hardly worth bothering with.
4 By carrying out in-depth evaluations some time after the training event a large amount of interesting data can be collected about the sales team.
5 Asking trainees what they want to see on a training event is an abdication of professional sales trainer accountability.
6 The only evaluation of a sales trainer worth having is that carried out by other trainers.
7 Sales training is meant to produce improved results, and it is this increase in results that will ultimately determine the effectiveness of the sales training programme.
8 Sales training cannot be effective unless line managers are accountable for picking up the responsibility for further field training immediately and continuously after the central training event.
9 Trainers should provide managers with objective feedback about the performance of trainees on centrally run training events.

Recommended reading

Bramley, P. 'Evaluating training', *Training Officer* July 1988.
Brandenburgh, D.C. 'Training evaluation', *Training & Development* Aug. 1982.
O'Shaughnessy, J. *Evaluate your Salesforce*, Management Publications 1984.

References

Cummings, W.T. 'Evaluating your salesforce', *Business* April 1984.
Hamblin, A.C. *Evaluation and Control of Training*, McGraw-Hill 1974.

Honeycutt, E.D. and T.H. Stevenson, 'Evaluating sales training programmes', *Industrial Marketing Management* 18. 1989.

O'Neill, H. 'Changing sales performance', *Training Officer* July 1983.

Phillips, J. *Handbook of Training Evaluation and Measurement Methods*, Kogan Page 1990.

10 Conclusions and suggested actions

More salespeople fail each day than succeed. Whose fault is that? A generation of 'macho'-style sales managers will say it is the salesperson's fault. They will say 'What these people need is commitment. What they need is guts. What they need is a kick up the backside'. If managers get really desperate they will say 'What they need is training' and pack them off to the training department as a last resort before firing them.

This attitude, while prevalent, fails to grasp the opportunities that are presented to us in the profession of selling, for a profession is exactly what it is. I realize that many people, whether at sales, sales management or sales training levels, do not treat it as such, but it is a profession nevertheless. I treat it as a profession and I would entreat those who read this book to follow the ideas it contains with an aim to improving the image of selling.

Selling has always had a bad press and suffers from a lack of understanding and an appreciation of its significant role in all our lives. Without salespeople, the economy would grind to a halt. Selling is the fuel for the economy and the life-blood of the nation.

I believe that in the world of selling there are a number of people who want to be professional, who want to succeed without resorting to trickery, who believe in what they do, but lack direction and especially good, clear sales management. There was a time when I blamed sales managers for this state of play, but while they are responsible for much that is wrong in the world of selling, managers themselves are merely a product of the same system. Most sales managers have taken the step toward management, not because they want to be managers, but because they do not want to be salespeople.

So where does the blame lie? I think it starts in schools, carries on in colleges, and ends with poor training. Schools never mention the role of selling in the economy, colleges overplay the marketing function—which excludes selling—and trainers hammer the final nail into the coffin by training salespeople in the wrong things.

Sales trainers are, of course, themselves a product of the system. They struggle with the impossible task of training people to sell in a hostile internal and external environment, when what salespeople need are good managers. Good sales training cannot hope to succeed without good managers. So where are they? I think they are there, somewhere, it's just that they are in hiding. In corporate Britain today, good managers are hiding behind a cloak of mystique, misinformation and ignorance about what makes a good salesperson, how to develop salespeople, and how to make good salespeople even better. Managers are being trained to expect that selection systems are available to identify good salespeople, that personnel departments have the ability to reward good salespeople appropriately, and that training departments are capable of developing the right skills to ensure sales success in salespeople.

All these beliefs are currently incorrect.

Structure

The biggest problem facing sales trainers is that in the vast majority of companies they have little or no power. In order to have training which works the following points with regard to structure need to be adopted:

- The training function must be equal to Finance and Marketing.
- The sales trainer must be able to implement training policies and procedures with authority not through negotiation.
- The procedures associated with training and development of sales staff must carry the same weight as the budgetary and control systems used by Finance.
- Sales training can add value to the bottom line through reducing labour turnover and increasing income. It should be judged, evaluated and reported on in this manner.

What do salespeople need to be trained to do?

The most important function that any salesperson has is to represent the company, its image, its products and services. To achieve this the following points should be borne in mind:

- Only employ people who already match the image you are seeking to portray.
- Accept that each company has a different sales role and therefore you need to teach people to sell for YOUR company, no matter how much previous experience they have.
- Recognize that the most dangerous and usually the salesperson most likely to fail is the one who knows it all, has done it all, and whose biggest sale has been in getting the job.
- Understand that sales success in another company is no guarantee of success in yours. Also understand and accept that failure in another company does not necessarily mean they will fail in yours.
- Regularly ask yourself and other senior managers what it is they want you to train salespeople to do. If it is impossible, say so.
- Calculate how long it will take to recoup the investment in training an individual and get agreement on the time-scale.
- Product knowledge will not guarantee success; it's important, but get

the balance right. Selling skills are more important than knowledge.
- The single most important element of success in selling is *attitude*. If potential salespeople come to you with the wrong attitude it will cost you a lot of money to put it right, and the chances of you succeeding are slim.

Sales trainers

The most significant element in any training programme or training event is the sales trainer. Getting the right person to deliver sales training is crucial to the company's success.

- All those involved in training salespeople or managing salespeople must be able to sell.
- The top salesperson does not always make the best sales trainer, but it is a good place to start looking for one.
- Every sales manager must be able to train salespeople.
- Sales training can only work if it is on-going and the only way that sales training can be on-going is if it is delivered daily by sales managers.
- Your primary task is to train the manager how to be a sales trainer.
- The central training programme should only be viewed as a foundation.
- If you hear 'Never mind what they teach you on the course, this is what happens in the real world', do something about it immmediately. Unless what happens on the training event is a reflection of what happens in the real world then it is pointless doing it.
- If you cannot get senior management support for the above points stop all sales training; otherwise it will be a waste of company resources, and you will be justified in making the Chairman aware of the waste.

The selling process

Selling is a clearly defined and simple process of finding people to sell to, contacting people, and selling yourself. The most difficult thing that salespeople have to do, after having found someone to sell to, is contacting prospects for an appointment. Anyone who does not have this as part of their sales role is not truly in selling—it is retailing or servicing. It is prospecting that causes the pressure and stress in selling.

- Salespeople have to receive regular sales training to help them overcome the rejection involved in prospecting.
- Salespeople must be encouraged to learn a lot about themselves.
- You have to teach your salespeople to adopt a flexible selling approach, and train your sales managers to recognize the difference.
- Your job and that of the sales manager, is to create an environment which fosters confidence in the salesperson.

Field training

No matter how good the central training programme is, it cannot hope to succeed without an effective field training programme to back it up.

- The primary function of any sales manager is as a coach to their sales team.
- Managers should be prepared to demonstrate to salespeople how to do a particular function of the job.
- Managers should keep a record of all training activity, and central trainers should agree with the managing director that these training records are part of the appraisal that is carried out on sales management effectiveness.
- All sales meetings must include a sales training element.

Motivation

Sales trainers play an important part in motivating salespeople to learn. Their influence is, however, restricted to the training event. Any lasting motivation can come only from the manager. It is certain that true motivation is self-motivation but having said that, people can be taught to develop self-motivation. It is an abdication of management responsibility to say that all you can hope to do is to create the ideal environment without understanding what this environment is.

- The ideal environment is one in which learning is continuous and everyone in the sales team understands that personal growth can never end.
- It is not impossible to change attitudes but it is very difficult.
- Begin by changing the behaviour of the salesperson.
- Sales training has to be an on-going process and salespeople must be allowed—and sometimes forced—to practice regularly.

Proving that sales training works

The ultimate purpose of your sales training is that it contributes substantially to the company's wealth. No matter how difficult it is to do, you must find a way to analyse the effects of your training programme and to prove that the company gets a good return on its investment. The longer you leave the process of concentrating on the results of your training, and the effect that it has on the bottom line, the more you will be susceptible to budgetary constraints. So:

- Monitor results before a programme.
- Keep a continuous system of data collection.
- Change the sales training to match current conditions before they change you. Sales training is a dynamic process and should change as often as the company, its products, and its services change.

Sales training can and does provide a bigger return on capital than any other form of corporate investment. The only thing stopping it in your company is you. I wish you success in your search for the sales training programme best suited to your company. It will not be easy, as each organization must develop its own unique programme. If this book motivates you to find that programme and stimulates a desire to be the best, then I will have succeeded in what I set out to do.

Appendices

Appendix 1
Post-course
evaluation

The company	agree	do not agree	50/50	not sure
I find the structure of the company extremely confusing.				
I think you need to get your act together between trainers and managers.				
I feel part of a team.				
All the things I was promised haven't happened.				
My targets are too high.				
There seems to be no training after the central programme.				
I do not feel that I am being developed.				
I have a clear plan of where I want to go, and the training I am getting is helping me to get there.				

Telephone sales technique	agree	do not agree	50/50	not sure
The training was excellent.				
I can't sell on the telephone.				
Too much time was spent on this on the course.				
My manager never spends enough time helping me to get this area of my sales technique right.				
The course content on this bears no relation to what actually happens in the field.				
Without training I would not have been as successful as I have been.				
The training dented what little confidence I have.				
I learned very little.				
I find it very difficult to put the theory into practice.				
All my colleagues who are successful do not use the technique learned on the course.				
There was not enough opportunity to practise this important area of selling.				

Selling skills	agree	do not agree	50/50	not sure
The theory on the course does not work in practice.				
We needed more about buyer behaviour.				
I can't get referred leads.				
I feel confident that I know what I am doing.				
The type of questioning technique we learned works extremely well.				
It's got nothing to do with selling technique. If they like me, they buy from me.				
Selling is easy in this environment—so sales training is superfluous.				
I wish I knew more about communication.				
People keep saying to me that they want to think about it and I can't seem to get them to make a decision.				
I need a lot more training.				
If the training had been better I would be a lot more successful.				
Too much time was spent on theory and not enough on role play.				
Without the training I doubt whether I would have been as successful.				
Field visits by my line manager are stressful.				

The problem with role play and visits by my line manager is that the situations are unreal.				
I need to review my sales skills regularly and practise them more with my colleagues at sales meetings.				
We just don't seem to spend enough time at sales meetings on sales training.				
On the occasions that I have not got the business, it is usually due to something I have done wrong.				

Product knowledge	agree	do not agree	50/50	not sure
I found the content confusing.				
I am able to remember most of it.				
There was too much to take in.				
The trainer's knowledge was very good.				
I feel confident that I know enough.				
The trainer explained everything to my satisfaction.				
We could have benefited from better materials and visuals.				
There should have been more formal testing.				
Product knowledge could have been covered by using self-study material.				

Structured selling	agree	do not agree	50/50	not sure
The theory is all right but it is impossible to put into practice.				
I have tried to do it as it was taught on the course and it works.				
The customers do not follow a structure and neither do I. It works my way.				
I found the training in this area very confusing.				
My manager does not use a structure when selling.				
My sales presentations seem to go on for hours—I just can't stop people talking.				
There are times when I haven't got a clue which part of the structure I am supposed to be in.				
Without a structure to my sales presentations I would not be as successful as I am.				
I think selling is a lot simpler than this theory of structure makes it.				

Attitude training	agree	do not agree	50/50	not sure
I felt confident when I left the course.				
I was not fooled by all the attitude building on the course.				
I have tried to stay positive but it is hopeless.				
My manager could seriously do with some attitude training.				
If it hadn't been for some of the attitude training on the central course I do not think I would have been as successful as I have been.				
I felt embarrassed by the attitude part of the talks—it might have been needed for some people, but leave me out.				
People who know me say I have changed.				
I just find all that positive mental attitude stuff a bit of a joke.				
I could do with some motivational tapes to listen to.				
The trainer was hopeless at all the attitude content of the course.				
I feel confident and positive; it's the manager who depresses me.				
Never mind attitude, it's hard work that counts.				

Body language	agree	do not agree	50/50	not sure
I thought this was all a bit far-fetched.				
I think it's important, but not that relevant.				
We did not spend enough time on the subject.				
The trainer seemed a bit unsure about the subject.				
I am so busy looking at body language I haven't got time to sell.				
It really works.				
It would take me a lifetime to learn how to read body language properly.				
When are you going to do some body language training for the managers—they need it!				
I need to go through this part of the course again.				
It is *what* you say that is important, not *how* you say it.				
All my customers have been negative in their body language, so it does not work for me.				

Time management	agree	do not agree	50/50	not sure
The course taught me nothing I did not know already.				
There is a big difference between theory and practice.				
Most of what was taught was irrelevant.				
I know the theory now, but I just can't seem to put it into practice.				
I found it very easy to get organized—I don't know what all the fuss is about.				
The session on time management was a waste of time.				
The trainer just confused me about all the methods to control your time.				
We didn't get enough help in organizing ourselves during the course, consequently my time management is a mess.				
It is not my time that needs managing, it is the manager's.				
There should have been a lot more time spent on this important subject.				
What we need are better diaries, not time management training.				
The problem with time is there isn't enough of it to do the things being asked of us.				

Appendix 2
Course,
expectation,
evaluation

Direct Sales Force
Three-Week Induction Sales Training Course

This course has been designed to include the following subject headings:

	A		B
Organizational structure/roles/aims			
Product knowledge and procedure			
Selling skills: theory			
Buyer behaviour			
Attitude and self-awareness			
Sales skills: practical			
Review and discussion periods			
	100%		

1 Please indicate in Column A what percentage of time, in your opinion, should be spent on these areas over the three-week period.
2 In Column B rate your opinion of yourself on a scale of 1 to 7, where 1 = poor knowledge and 7 = competent.

_____

Signature (optional)

Appendix 3
Allocation of course time

As a group, when asked to indicate what % of time you felt should be spent on various areas, you came up with the following:

		A	B
1	Product knowledge and procedure	18%	
2	Attitude and self-awareness	17%	
3	Selling skills: theory	15%	
4	Selling skills: practice	14%	
5	Buyer behaviour	14%	
6	Review and discussion periods	12%	
7	Organizational structure and aims	10%	

If you wish to recommend any change to your group decision, please indicate in Column B.

Appendix 4
Evaluation of trainees

Trainee.. Trainer .... Date................

Describe the image portrayed and whether this fits that required by the company.

How effectively did the trainee assimilate information about the company's products and services?

Is it necessary for the trainee to change the way he/she delivers our sales message and, if so, how?

What changes and improvements in sales behaviours have you noticed in the trainee during the training event?

What are your positive evaluations about the trainee?

What concerns do you have about the trainee?

What objective data can you supply that would confirm or question this employment decision?

Index